Dear Jami,

Of all while been & heard you are as beautiful yo... inside as you are outside. Yo... very special to me & you ha... much potential. Never settle for less.

Much love.
Sister Moore

MISS AMERICA

Sharlene Wells
MISS AMERICA

Sheri L. Dew

Deseret Book Company
Salt Lake City, Utah

First printing November 1985

Library of Congress Cataloging-in-Publication Data

Dew, Sheri L.
    Sharlene Wells, Miss America.

    1. Wells, Sharlene, 1964–   . 2. Beauty contestants
—Utah—Biography. 3. Miss America Pageant, Atlantic
City, N.J. 4. Mormons—Utah—Biography. I. Title.
HQ1220.U5D47 1985   305.4'079 [B]   85-20708
ISBN 0-87579-012-7

To the youth of the Church

Contents

Preface

I still remember driving home one Saturday afternoon; the date was September 15, 1984, to be exact. I was only vaguely aware of the radio until the newscaster announced that Miss Utah, Sharlene Wells, was one of the ten finalists for that evening's Miss America pageant.

Although I knew only a few specifics about Sharlene, I certainly knew who she was. She was the reigning Miss Utah, BYU homecoming queen, Holiday Bowl queen, a former Utah Junior Miss, and a daughter of Elder Robert E. Wells of the First Quorum of the Seventy, The Church of Jesus Christ of Latter-day Saints. Associates at the publication where I work had encouraged me to publish an article about LDS pageant winners. I had resisted, insisting that readers expected more from us than reports on beauty pageants.

Perhaps you can tell that I have never put much stock in the beauty pageant system and, by inference, beauty pageant contestants. I have tended to dismiss bathing beauties with a wave of the hand and the notion that, collectively, they rely too much on looks and not nearly enough on brains, personality, talent, and character.

Nevertheless, I found myself watching the Miss America pageant that evening (a first for me), and I admit that, despite my preconceived bias, I was thrilled when Gary Collins called out Sharlene's name as the new Miss America. It almost seemed like a blow for the little man, or girl—a girl from Utah, and a member of the Church, no less.

Even more, I was delighted at the prospects of an LDS Miss America. In our culture, only a few women have occasion to be seen and heard on a national let alone international spectrum, and suddenly Sharlene had landed smack dab in the middle of the limelight. If she represented herself well, I reasoned, there was no telling what impact she might have. The very next morning, at her first official news conference, as Sharlene endorsed conservative and traditional values and proudly claimed her membership in the Church, I smiled to myself, feeling somehow a claim on this girl who had the gumption to boldly declare morals that were far from chic in today's world. I was impressed with her candor, self-confidence, and savvy.

A few weeks later, I found myself on a plane headed for Los Angeles, where I was to interview Sharlene for a cover story in *This People* magazine. I was curious about what I would find in a face-to-face conversation with her. After a morning together, I was pleasantly surprised. She was, to coin a timely phrase, more than a pretty face, as comfortable in Levis with feet propped up on a table as she was when dolled up for the photographer. I found her to be bright, informed, disarmingly honest, and a far cry from the prima donna I had half expected.

Several months later, Deseret Book's president Ron Millett approached me about writing a book-length treatment of Sharlene's year as Miss America. I was hesitant. It is dangerous to write about someone who is alive. There are two inherent dangers: the temptation to glorify, or the overprotective urge to understate. Objectivity can be elusive.

On the other hand, I felt Sharlene was one of the best role models for young women to come along in a long time. It seemed to me that her story ought to be told, and I agreed to handle the project.

Undoubtedly, some will feel much as I did initially. "Why spotlight a beauty queen when there are thousands out there who are making *bona fide* contributions to society?" The question is valid, but after dozens of interviews with Sharlene and others who know her best, I have arrived at a conclusion—one I'd like to spell out.

Sharlene Wells is not without flaw, and any attempt to represent her accordingly would be unfair to her and misleading to readers. In some ways, she is much like any other twenty-one-year-old woman. She has many of the same hopes, desires, moods, and challenges. She is not the most gorgeous girl I have ever met, nor the brightest nor the most talented. She is, however, exceptionally bright, highly talented, very attractive, and poised beyond her years. She is perhaps the most composite, well-rounded young woman I have known.

What is this leading to? Very simply, an author's biased observation. There are those in this day and age who bow and bend like a willow in a windstorm to the distractions of the eighties; those who say morality and character are unenlightened, out of vogue, and terribly provincial. There are those who have been exposed to the truth but are embarrassed to espouse it; those who fritter life away because they're embarrassed to take a stand; those who hesitate to speak out because it would be socially detrimental; those who say the gospel is confining, and that the Church's stringent moral code is unfashionable; those content to sit back while others make the world go round; and those who believe they can eat, drink, and be merry today and worry about the consequences later.

To all these individuals, especially women who struggle with themselves and their identity, I unhesitatingly recommend Sharlene Wells as a realistic role model. She has known what it is like to be on the outside looking in, what it's like to be mocked by friends, the sensation of living around the world and having few opportunities to put down roots. She has worked to build her testimony. She has learned to make good choices. And though she has weaknesses, and is the first to acknowledge them, she is delightfully solid in substantial ways.

Sharlene has a wonderful grasp on perspective, on what is important and what is not. She understands one simple but pervasive fact. She is where she is because of *who* she is. Sharlene Wells is a product of her environment, and her environment is, very simply, the gospel.

You can be beautiful, fun-loving, studious, intelligent, and talented and still keep the commandments. You can mix and mingle in today's world and stay committed to principles. You can succeed, whatever that word really means, without sacrificing values. You can speak out in behalf of all that is good and right and have national and even international impact. You needn't apologize, ever, for who you are, or what you believe. Because in the 1980s, sitting on fences is definitely out of vogue.

It is much too early to measure Sharlene Wells's influence on the Church, her home state, the country, or the world. By some, she will be remembered as the Miss America who "saved" the pageant, though she doesn't see herself that way. To others, she will be an irritating recollection of a goody two shoes. But for now, she is a bright moment in a world confused about the role of women. For that reason, I am pleased to have participated in bringing her story to print.

Acknowledgments

When Sharlene Wells and in essence the Wells family agreed to this project they in all likelihood had no idea how time consuming that commitment would prove. Despite what I'm sure was often an untimely inconvenience, Sharlene, Helen, and Elder Robert Wells made themselves available virtually upon request. I am grateful for their patient hours of cooperation through what proved to be dozens of hours of interview. They also provided me with literally boxes of letters, newspaper clippings, journals, and photographs, all of which proved invaluable and reduced the number of additional research hours required.

I am also grateful to the professionals at Deseret Book who have handled this project in expeditious fashion—in particular to Ron Millett and Eleanor Knowles, who conceptualized the project, and to editor Marci Chapman, who refined the finished product and made the enterprise less painful than it might have been.

Finally, I must mention my mom and dad. They always said I'd thank them for those piano lessons. I have, but I appreciate their emphasis on education as well. To them goes any credit.

Chapter 1

A New Miss America

It was well past midnight on the East Coast. Backstage at Atlantic City's Convention Center, in a large room that nevertheless seemed small and stuffy, waves of noisy people pushed their way closer to the front and jockeyed for position. Photographers tested flashes and straightened tripods; reporters talked loudly to be heard above the din and TV crews quickly set up equipment and covered the floor with a maze of railroad-track-like cords. A guard stood watch at the door, carefully screening everyone who entered. Other officious-looking individuals—working to make sense of the mayhem—steered some two hundred members of the press, dignitaries, and others to their appointed spots. Security was tight. Parents and immediate family could enter. Friends could not. Members of the press with specific credentials were welcome; all others were left to stand in the hall.

Suddenly, the hubbub quieted for a moment as a group of escorts surrounding a young woman entered and took their places on a small podium. At the center of attention, encircled by microphones and curious reporters, was a tall, slender strawberry blonde. Her makeup was a bit streaked, and a rhinestone-studded crown balanced on her head. For just a moment, she looked almost bewildered.

After all, only a week earlier she'd been just another coed majoring in broadcast journalism at Brigham Young University. Just an hour or so earlier, she'd been but one of fifty-one talented young women competing in the Miss

America pageant. But these girls and this particular pageant were unusual in at least one significant way. Coming on the heels of the stormiest scandal in Miss America's sixty-four-year history, the selection of Miss America 1985 was of particular interest to skeptical Eastern reporters and press around the world who sniffed the scent of a crumbling institution, and who wondered and doubted if the pageant could redeem itself. So when, just minutes earlier, Gary Collins had announced, "And the new Miss America is Miss Utah!" and Sharlene Wells had walked the length of the Convention Center's 134-foot runway while Collins sang "She's Our Miss America" in tribute, her life had taken a dizzying and irrevocable turn.

Now, as lights flashed with stacatto-like frequency, reporters began firing questions at her. It was bedlam, an intimidating situation for anyone, but Sharlene quickly raised her hands and laid ground rules. "Just a minute," she half-shouted. "Just a minute, please. I can't answer more than one question at once. Now," she paused, singling out a reporter on the front row, "what's *your* question?"

The journalist—surprised to be picked out of the noise—paused then asked, "How do you feel about the youth of America?"

"There are wonderful youth in America today, but I'd like to see a return to traditional standards."

"What do you mean by traditional standards?" an onslaught of reporters asked at once.

"Please, I will only answer one question at a time," she insisted again, "and I will indicate the person that I want."

Sharlene took charge, directing traffic. There was an intensity in the room, an anxiousness to find out just what kind of girl this new Miss America was. As one reporter after another shot volleys of point-blank questions at the young woman, she returned fire with a barrage of direct, no-nonsense answers.

Walter A. Snyder

At the press conference immediately after the Miss America pageant

"Did your religion have anything to do with your selection?"

"I certainly hope so," Sharlene answered. "I live my religion seven days a week."

"How do you feel about the Mormon Church's stand on women?"

"Women have an important role in the Mormon Church. Women are on an equal standing. They have never been second-class citizens. I am, however, a woman of the eighties, and I have a career in mind."

"Then what's your position on the Equal Rights Amendment?"

"I am in favor of women's rights, but I do not support the Equal Rights Amendment because the wording of the amendment itself is too vague. We have no idea how courts will interpret those eighteen words, and women's rights are already protected under the Fourteenth Amendment. The Equal Rights Amendment would make us a neuter society."

"What about prayer in the classroom?"

"God should never have been banned from the schools. Our nation was founded on religious freedom."

"Back to the traditional values you mentioned, what do you mean by that?"

"I mean no drugs, no profanity, no sex outside of marriage. And the deterioration of the family is one of my greatest concerns."

"What are your views on abortion?"

"Life is precious. Abortion takes away the birthright everyone has."

"Would you ever pose in the nude?"

"Absolutely not."

"How do you feel about premarital sex?"

"Sex should be confined to the bonds of marriage."

A sophisticated female reporter from the back of the room interrupted, "But what if you're thirty-five, unmarried, and a professional woman?"

"Then you are thirty-five, unmarried, a professional woman, and still no premarital sex. Next question," Sharlene shot back.

And on it went, with dozens of questions skirting the issue of her predecessor's indiscretions. When finally questioned directly about the circumstances surrounding Vanessa Williams's problems, Sharlene answered, "Vanessa is a talented, beautiful girl who was an exceptional Miss America. What happened was a tragedy. As far as it relates to me, I'm a Mormon from Utah. That should say it all. I've kept my life above reproach. I have no skeletons in my closet."

As the press conference continued, muffled comments could be heard around the room. "She's right. She's absolutely right." "Isn't this great." "Do you think she's for real?" "Aw, come on. Nobody believes this stuff these days." "It's refreshing to have somebody like this back as Miss America." At least twice, the journalists broke into loud applause.

A number of reporters made their way to the side of the room where Sharlene's parents, Robert and Helen Wells, were standing. One man said to Robert Wells, "She sounds more like a lawyer than a Miss America." Another commented, "I've been covering the Miss America pageant for twenty years, and she's the most articulate Miss America I've ever seen." A third said simply, "She's no airhead. She really knows where she's going." Still another added, "Boy, she's got her head on straight. What a fresh approach."

One reporter who identified himself as being from the Bible Belt pulled Robert Wells aside and said, "I was so discouraged about last year's scandal. I came here fasting and praying for a new Miss America who would set the standards again, and my prayers have been answered."

Even Robert Wells was amazed at his daughter's handling of the situation. "I knew Sharlene was intelligent, because she had always had good grades. I knew she was spiritual, because you can feel that in a person. But I had never seen her in that kind of a setting, and my first reaction was, 'She's grown up.' Her answers were better than anything I could have given. No one has any idea what kind of girl has been chosen until the first press conference, and in that demanding situation Sharlene had total composure. She was more magnified at that instance than at any other. She was equal to that challenging responsibility."

If Sharlene's first encounter with the press was anything, it was forthright. Her answers to tough questions were direct, firm, at times bordering on tactless, and left nothing to the imagination. They also left her no "out." How many twenty-year-old women would or could make the unequivocable statement, "I have lived my life above reproach"?

In the wee hours of the morning, as Sharlene Wells, Miss America 1985, made her way to her hotel suite, puzzled journalists flooded the news wires with stories about a Miss America who didn't drink or smoke; who denounced pre-marital sex; who spoke avidly against the Equal Rights Amendment and abortion; who supported prayer in the classroom; and who even suggested that the pageant's swim-suit competition could just as well be held in private.

The next morning headlines around the world intro-duced Sharlene Wells:

"A Squeaky Clean Miss America" (*USA Today*)

"Mormon Queen *Rescues* American Morality" (from a leading Swiss newspaper)

"Miss America '85 Called Almost Too Good to be True" (*Houston Chronicle*)

"A Mormon Girl from Paraguay is Miss America" (a newspaper in Lima, Peru)

"New Miss America Wants Restoration of Values" (from an Amarillo, Texas, paper)

"A Beauty from Utah Wins Studded Crown of Miss America 1985" (*Deseret News*, Salt Lake City, Utah)

An editorial opinion published in the *Las Vegas Sun* seems to typify early impressions: "Here she comes. The epitome of motherhood and apple pie. Yes, Sharlene Wells, the new Miss America, represents the kind of good old-fashioned values that the country's most famous beauty pageant strives to portray. This time it looks like contestant officials won't have to worry about another scandal which cost last year's Miss America, Vanessa Williams, her crown. The twenty-year-old Miss Wells is a Sunday School teacher in the LDS Church. She doesn't smoke, drink, or gamble. She doesn't believe in premarital sex, and she opposes abor-tion and the Equal Rights Amendment. For a pageant marked by national controversy in recent months, some

would say the selection of Miss Wells is almost divine inter-
vention" (19 September 1984).

In press conferences the following day, Sharlene again
stated her position on major issues. Her answers continued
to be snappy and decisive. During one session, a female reporter spotted Helen Wells standing toward the back and
approached her with a question. "Mrs. Wells, these values
Sharlene expounds are beautiful. But tell me, since you
probably know her better than anyone else, is all this for
real? Isn't this a put on for the press?"

The doubter wasn't the only skeptical member of the
press. Toward the end of one press conference a reporter in-
quired, "Well, haven't you done *anything* you might be

Fielding questions from reporters the morning after she
was crowned Miss America

ashamed of?" There was a long pause. When Sharlene finally spoke, she said, somewhat apologetically, "No . . . No, there's nothing major that I can think of." The way she put it, it seemed to be the first question that had stumped her all weekend.

From the beginning, late the evening of September 15, 1984, as Sharlene Wells took the traditional stroll down the Convention Center runway while a capacity crowd of some twenty-one thousand stood and cheered enthusiastically, and later as the nation caught its first glimpse of the spirited pageant winner, it was apparent that her reign as Miss America would be distinctive. This was a girl who was anxious to speak her mind, though her views were incompatible with many of the day's liberal mores; yet she struck a responsive chord with traditionalists. Even more, she was a girl who at least appeared to practice what she preached. She was one of the first Miss Americas born outside the United States, only the second Utahn and Mormon to be crowned Miss America, and the first daughter of a General Authority of The Church of Jesus Christ of Latter-day Saints to be so honored.

Of course, the world didn't realize just what that meant. But where did it all begin? Anyone who met her would find that she was, in fact, an unusual girl—one whose roots were both highly typical and very unusual. And one who just might prove to be, at least for a year, America's most exceptional miss.

Chapter 2

She Must Have Been
a Beautiful Baby

Late in the night, on March 16, 1964, in a Seventh Day
Adventist hospital in Asunción, Paraguay, Robert and
Helen Wells became the parents of a healthy baby girl. They
named her Sharlene. She had four older brothers and sisters:
Dana, David, Bobby, and Susan. Two other sisters, Elayne
and Janet, would follow.

Helen vividly remembers her first impression of her
daughter. "She was an exact replica of her father. My first
thought was, 'How strange for a baby girl to look like her
dad.'" (Twenty years later, after his daughter had made national headlines, Robert Wells would have an ironic, considering Sharlene's early likeness to him, encounter in a Salt
Lake City department store. "I presented my credit card to
make a purchase. The clerk looked at my identification and
said, 'Robert E. Wells. Are you Miss America's father?'
With a display of some pride, I said I was. The clerk looked
down again at my card, then back up at my weather-beaten
face and said, 'She must have a beautiful mother.'")

As Citibank's senior officer in Paraguay, Robert Wells
enjoyed a close association with diplomats and dignitaries in
the capital city. When he learned that the British ambassador had a daughter who was a nurse, he asked Helen if she
wouldn't like the girl to help with the baby for the first few
weeks. Helen agreed and arrangements were made.

It wasn't long, though, before she regretted the decision.
"Each time Sharlene would cry," she remembers, "this En-

Sharlene, three days old, with her father

glish nurse would run and attend to her, and Sharlene learned awfully quick that she needed only to cry and some-one would pick her up."

The nurse was dismissed, but not before an annoying precedent had been set. "My wife is infuriated with me when I say this, but although babies are cute and cuddly, they are vegetables to me until they begin to communicate," Robert Wells says. "Remembering her in the vegetable state, Shar-lene was the cryingest baby we ever had. But she didn't cry when she was rocked, so we'd rock her all night long. We had a cradle by the bed, and I could rock it with my foot until she'd go to sleep. I'd sleep for awhile until she woke again, then I'd wake up and rock her until I went to sleep again. She was a very difficult baby to please. She was happy in the daytime, but she'd cry all night. *Every* night."

When Sharlene was seven months old, the Wells family took a vacation to the United States—Disneyland and Las Vegas, in particular. "Even then," Helen remembers, "Shar-lene cried much of the night. We didn't want to disturb the other guests in the hotel, so Bob would take her for a ride in the car. She'd calm down and be perfectly quiet, but when he'd bring her back to the room, she'd start to cry again. It wasn't until she was about a year old that she calmed down at night."

And that was just the beginning. Early on, the Wellses realized that their little tow-headed girl was going to give them a run for their money. Sharlene likes to describe herself as "curious." Her father puts it another way. "As soon as Sharlene got to the stage where she was talking and walking, she was delightful. But she did have an unusual ability to do destructive things. She did more damage to more things than her older brothers did."

On one occasion Robert took his daughter with him on a quick errand, leaving Sharlene in the car as he dashed inside to meet a friend. During the two or three minutes he was gone, Sharlene located and opened a toolbox, selected a hammer, and watched the safety glass break into small crystals as she pounded out the car windows.

And that was just a beginning. She yanked the arm of a stereo off. She tried to ride a television cart, pulling over an expensive television set and destroying it beyond repair. The technician said he had never seen a set so thoroughly ruined. She located a small bottle of kerosene that had been accidentally left open and drank it—and nearly died.

Helen says she'll never forget one afternoon when she was standing in the backyard of their Cordoba, Argentina, home. Suddenly she heard the two-year-old Sharlene squeal, "Mommy, Mommy, look at me." She looked around, then behind. Her heart sank as she finally looked up to see Sharlene draped like a flour sack over the third-floor balcony. That time Sharlene's older brother rescued her.

"From the beginning I wondered what we had on our hands," Helen admits. "Most babies crawl, then stand, and

Sharlene, three years old, with big sister Dana

finally take their first step. But Sharlene never walked. When she got up on her two feet, she let go of the wall and ran across the room. She has always had an insatiable curiosity about everything. I remember taking Sharlene to the zoo when she was only three or four years old. It was an incredible experience that clued us in to what we were in for. She could not see things fast enough. We *ran* to see the monkeys; we *ran* to the elephants. We could not keep up with her. It was as though she were running out of time and had to make sure she saw everything. In short, Sharlene was not a docile child. We could never anticipate what she'd do next."

But though she was rambunctious and entirely unpredictable, the Wellses soon found that Sharlene had redeeming qualities. Even as a little girl, she was perpetually happy. "After she got past that initial crying stage," Robert Wells recalls, "once she could talk and move around, she was a very happy girl—always happy. That was one of her most obvious characteristics from age two on. Maybe when she

Sharlene, five months old, with her mother in Paraguay

was little she was just frustrated being in a body that couldn't do anything."

Even when she was tiny, Sharlene did respond to one thing—music. "When Sharlene was just three or four months old," Helen says, "Bob would hold her in his arms as though they were waltzing, and put her arm around his neck, and they would dance. She would hold her back straight and laugh and laugh. She loved music."

It may have been her musical bent that made Sharlene a natural on stage. Some would have called her precocious. At age two, her mother remembers taking her to watch her older brother and sister, David and Dana, take their Argentine folk-dancing lessons. "Sharlene would sit on the sidelines and tap her feet to the music. When the lesson was finished, she'd get up on the dance floor and imitate what her older brother and sister had been doing. It was amazing. She could do those intricate dance steps."

As early as preschool, she loved being center stage. "She

went to a little preschool in Quito, Ecuador, and from the beginning she loved to participate in programs of any kind," Helen says. "She never seemed to mind getting up in front of an audience."

There has always been a great deal of music in the Wells home. Helen Wells is an accomplished concert pianist who has accompanied many singers and instrumentalists. "We always had people in the house who were practicing for performances," Robert says. "Sharlene grew up hearing good music, seeing the rehearsing and practicing, and apparently decided very early that that was good."

In those early years, Sharlene found any number of things to her liking. Her curiosity and propensity for adventure fit in perfectly at the Wells household, because the Wellses' way of life was anything but typical. By the time she was four, Sharlene had lived in Paraguay, Argentina, Ecuador, and Mexico, and she'd been exposed to an affluent, diverse, and constantly changing environment. Because of her father's professional stature as a highly respected international banker, she and the rest of the family were constantly thrown into new and changing situations.

Robert Wells functioned as the senior officer in the field for Citibank in various South American countries. "I not only managed all of the different branches of the bank, but was responsible for our relationships with the host government, embassies, and major international businesses who operated in the country. There was a great deal of diplomatic and public relations work involved, because many of those countries borrowed heavily from our New York office." Because Citibank is the granddaddy of the South American banking community, Robert Wells's position afforded him great visibility and prestige. He hobnobbed on a regular basis with wealthy businessmen, politicians, and other men of influence—playing polo with clients, anchoring his sailboat at the local yacht club, flying his own plane, and counseling regularly on economic affairs with local government officials who sought his advice. Everything that affected the host country's economic tide fell into his area of interest.

Robert Wells's prominence extended to his family, though the "living-in-a-glass-bowl syndrome did not extend too much to the children," Helen insists. Both Helen and her husband admit, however, that their children did adapt to a life-style that included maids, large residences, and numerous other accoutrements of success. "Sharlene and the other children saw us going out to a lot of parties and hosting everything from small sit-down dinners to parties of five hundred guests," Robert Wells says. "And her friends were the children of diplomats and financiers and international businessmen."

"Though we made it a point to introduce our children to people who visited our home," Helen says, "our social life with Citibank was restricted to late-evening functions, so the children were usually not involved. We did, however, have the financial resources to afford them certain opportunities—such as visiting other countries and taking interesting vacations. They certainly saw things they never would have if we'd been living in Salt Lake City all that time."

It's possible that all of the wealth and prominence had only a nominal effect on the very young Sharlene Wells—in part, at least, because the Wells family's way of life changed drastically when she was but four years old. At that time, her father was called to serve as president of the Mexico Monterrey Mission. Robert Wells took a leave of absence from Citibank, and the family moved to Monterrey. It is of those days in Mexico that Sharlene has her earliest memories.

Though she remembers their home as being "huge and gorgeous," and recalls also that she had her own maid, this change in environment would prove to permanently remove the Wellses from their stratified life-style.

Six-year-old Sharlene ready for her school program in Monterrey, Mexico

In Mexico, Sharlene had "crushes on the missionaries," went to kindergarten and first grade in Mexico, and learned to speak English and Spanish. She doesn't remember there being a difference between languages. "We spoke English in the home, but they taught Spanish and English in the schools." She spoke Spanish with the maids, and as early as age two and a half conversed well in the language. One of the last things she remembers about Mexico is standing with her family at the airport where dozens of missionaries had gathered to send them off.

"The missionaries kept telling me, 'Don't forget your Spanish.' On the way to the airport, they sang 'There Is an Hour of Peace and Rest' in Spanish, and to this day, I can't remember the English words to that song."

Chapter 3

Life in Salt Lake City

After giving Robert Wells, one of their key officers in the field, a three-year leave of absence, Citibank wanted him back. But the prestigious international lending institution wasn't the only organization that came calling. In 1971, near the conclusion of Robert Wells's term as president of the Mexico Monterrey Mission, President N. Eldon Tanner asked if he wouldn't forego a return to Citibank and instead move his family to Salt Lake City, where there was an opening as director of the Church's Central Purchasing department. "We fasted and prayed about the opportunities," Robert Wells confides, "and at somewhat of a sacrifice in salary and social status, we accepted a humble Church position."

For one reason or another, the Wellses found the adjustment to Salt Lake City trying. "We are perhaps somewhat critical of the social milieu here," Robert confesses, "because both times we've moved to Utah our children have had trouble making friends. Part of that may have been that we were used to having a lot of attention given to us in banking and in the mission field. Perhaps here our children were just being treated normal, and they didn't recognize that. But we were all used to the Latin American environment, which is very affectionate. In Salt Lake City, we didn't find immediate affection and acceptance, which we thought we would."

At the time of the move, Sharlene was in the second

grade, and for the first time, her life took on a normal pattern. On the other hand, her personality suffered. Suddenly she wasn't the same happy child her parents had come to expect. Sharlene readily admits that grade school and junior high left something to be desired, and that she suffered from a rash of childhood and adolescent handicaps.

She had a lisp. Helen Wells chuckles, apparently enjoying the irony of a future Miss America with a lisp, as she recalls, "I was concerned because Sharlene could not say her s's. I approached her second grade teacher, Susan Hinckley, about it, and she told me she'd see what she could do."

Only a week or so later, Sharlene came bounding home from school one afternoon and announced proudly, "Listen to me. I don't have a lisp anymore." "And she didn't," Helen says. "We could tell then that when Sharlene put her mind to something, she was all business." (Twelve years later, Sharlene's second grade teacher would write, "You can never know how excited I was to watch my little student be-

Sharlene (right), eight years old, with her sister Elayne

come Miss America. I remember you as being serious, conscientious, independent, prompt, and persistent. These qualities just had to lead you to this important stepping-stone in your life.")

Determination and persistence, unfortunately, had little to do with looks, and Sharlene poignantly remembers feeling as though she were sorely lacking in that area. She had a wide A-shaped gap, which she describes as "a space big enough to drive a truck through," between her front teeth. In general, she felt that she was plain-Jane, an impression that was apparently justified according to Robert Wells. "Helen scolds me for this, but there was a time when I looked on her as a bit of an ugly duckling. She was homely in those early years, and that's all there was to it."

The tall and leggy Sharlene was also a tomboy who could run, swim, and play soccer with the best of them—even with the best of the boys. She confesses to "never playing girls' games. I wasn't familiar with what other girls did." Because of that, she was "one of the guys." Her father says, "From very early years, she loved to play ball with the boys and compete as one of them. She was tall and fast. She loved Levis and ponytails, which is still kind of a signature to her. We started out shortening her name from Sharlene to Sharly, and as she became more and more boyish, we changed that to Charlie."

Though Charlie was right in the middle of things on the soccer field, socially she seemed to be perpetually on the outside looking in. As she describes it, "I didn't have much initiative when it came to social things, because I wasn't popular. That's all there was to it. And I was *very* insecure about that. I was always befriending the underdog, the girl who no one else wanted to have anything to do with. And you know why? Because I felt that I was an underdog, too.

"Before I went to South America the second time, I was a follower. I was definitely not a leader. I guess I always held

my own, but I watched the world go by. The other kids held
the offices; the other kids got involved in things; the other
kids were popular; the other kids had friends. While we were
living in Salt Lake City, and I was in junior high, I never
took the initiative to get involved. I didn't have the confidence to." Sharlene did venture out to one junior high
dance, which confirmed her worst suspicions. "I felt like a
complete loser. Nobody would dance with me. I stood by
myself all night."

One problem that may have separated Sharlene from her
peers was her propensity for talking about South America,
about her family, and about herself. Her mother says, "She
had a problem with coming across as self-centered. One of
her teachers in the Young Women's program called me one
day and said, 'Your daughter has had so many experiences,
and they are interesting. I love to hear them. But you may
want to talk to Sharlene about not talking about them so
much because it's intimidating to the girls.' I did talk to
Sharlene, but I don't think much of it got through because

Sharlene with her dog, Pupsie

Back row: David, Robert L., Susan, Dana; front row: Elayne, Elder Wells, Janet, Sister Wells, Sharlene

several years later, when we came back from South America a second time, I would hear her talking much the same way. She was so thrilled about everything she'd been able to experience, but her friends didn't take it that way."

Sharlene admits that it was hard for her to adjust to the United States. "I kept wanting to talk about South America, and after a while the kids my age started saying, 'Would you quit talking about that place?'"

Despite the discouraging aspects of childhood and early adolescence, things weren't totally gloomy. During her grade school years some interesting personality traits and qualities began to quietly emerge. When it came to schoolwork, Sharlene was a bright star, and it was obvious that she had a natural talent for music in general and the piano in particular. In fact, from her earliest school days teachers raved about how quick she was to catch on to things. "I don't remember ever feeling that I couldn't hold my own academically," Sharlene says. "Even though I didn't have many friends, I felt on the ball academically, and that helped." She also remembers having crushes on some of the boys her age. "I was so awkward in trying to get their attention. If you can imagine this, about the only thing I could think of to say to them was, 'Do you want me to help you with your math?'"

As it turns out, Sharlene was a little smoother at the piano than she was at playing up to boys. At age seven, she started taking piano lessons from her mother. Sharlene says, "Mom decided there was no more agency, that we were going to learn to play the piano, and that was that." When asked what she remembers most about growing up in the Wells household, Sharlene immediately answers, "Practicing, practicing, practicing. I learned that if I wanted to get my way, all I had to do was practice on my own, and Mom would let me do pretty much whatever I wanted."

Her memory may be vague on that score, but perhaps without realizing it, her comment draws attention to some other qualities that began to surface early. Her mother and father both say Sharlene was still in grade school when they realized she was a determined, disciplined, obedient, and maybe even stubborn girl. "I never had to push her or remind her to, for example, say her prayers or practice the piano," Helen Wells explains. "Once she started on something, she went at it full steam."

"She was an excellent student," her father adds. "All of her teachers were very high on her as a dedicated student who was quick to learn. But she was also stubborn when it came to sticking up for her own rights. Even back then, she loved to be identified with a cause."

There was one more thing that evidenced itself. Despite the disappointing, low moments at school and with friends, Sharlene had a built-in chuckle. Says her father, "We called it the Charlie chuckle. She was always laughing. Sharlene responds with humor to almost anything, and she has what must be an inborn positive reaction to things. She is perpetually happy."

Sharlene responded very positively to her father's call, in October 1976, to the First Quorum of the Seventy. And though Sharlene says she didn't fully realize at the time just how significant that was, she did have the sneaking suspicion and hope that it would mean returning to South America. "I was thrilled about that, because I really missed it, and because I didn't fit in up here in the United States."

She got her wish, and as a seventh grader, she and her family headed south.

Chapter 4

Return to South America

While most girls her age were still stumbling over the pronunciations of places whose significance were associated exclusively with the next geography quiz, Sharlene was living them firsthand. Rio, São Paulo, Santiago, Buenos Aires—the names alone evoke images of narrow mountain passages, exotic wildlife, colorful and ancient customs, and untamed jungles. Though age thirteen is a typically disastrous, temperamental age to be uprooted, for Sharlene, her return to South America was literally a godsend.

The Wellses' first stop in February 1977 was in Santiago, Chile, where initially conditions were inconvenient. Elder Wells went south first to find a place to live and to get acquainted with his new assignment as area supervisor of the Southern Cove of South America, which included Chile and Argentina. Uruguay and Paraguay were added six months later. He found, however, that tuition to the American schools was atrociously expensive. It appeared that, at least for the time being, the only alternative was to have Helen, herself a former schoolteacher, tutor the three girls—Sharlene, Elayne, and Janet—at home. The arrangement left something to be desired.

"Bob told me about the problem before we left for Chile, and I enrolled the girls in the Calvert home study course and ordered all the books. Bob borrowed three desks from the Church there, and we put one in each of their bedrooms. The girls would spend most of the day studying in their rooms, and I'd go from room to room trying to help them. We didn't have a yard, so sometimes we'd go down the street and play ball in the wide islands in the middle of the street. It really was a sad situation."

More worrisome to Helen than the makeshift school conditions was Sharlene's initial adjustment. "I was concerned about Sharlene during those days. It was one of the few times she did little more than the minimum, and she didn't seem able to articulate very well. It was probably the teacher."

Before long, the Wells family was transferred to Buenos Aires. Simultaneously, they received permission from Church headquarters to enroll the children in the Lincoln American School, which was a relatively small but academically challenging school that had an extremely diverse cultural and religious cross section.

"In this school," Robert Wells explains, "our children associated with children of diplomats, international financiers, and prominent Argentine businessmen. Their friends were Orientals, Europeans, blacks, Argentines, North Americans, and schoolmates from all walks of life. Some of Sharlene's friends were Jewish, others were Greek Orthodox, some were of the Islamic faith. One of her best friends was the son of the Saudi Arabian ambassador, who was from the royal house of Saudi."

In the beginning, Sharlene held back a little and didn't "jump in with both feet," as Helen Wells remembers it. "She's always had some reserve, and it wasn't easy for her to be friendly and warm with people she didn't know." Additionally, she retained a nagging lack of self-confidence, a throwback to her earlier school experiences in Salt Lake City.

"At first, when Sharlene would come home from school," Helen says, "she wasn't as happy as I'd have liked her to be. I'd ask her how things had gone that day, and she'd answer, 'Oh, fine.' 'Are you making friends?' 'Not really. They don't seem to accept me.' Then one day she came bouncing home and said, 'I'm so happy. I've found the best friend in the world.' I asked her who it was, and she said, 'I went into the library and discovered all those books, and I'm going to spend as much time as I can reading.'"

It wasn't long, though, before Sharlene's fate began to change. When she finally came out of her shell, she exploded. It was the good luck of a sweepstakes winner, uncanny timing, or perhaps much more than that—depending on how you care to look at it—that gave her the nudge she needed.

The Lincoln American School, like any other school system, had its share of cliques. But because tuition was very expensive and most of its students were the sons and daughters of diplomats, military officers, and businessmen, it was also small and very transient. Students came and went at an amazing clip. Sharlene felt this was a stroke of luck. "When I moved in to the Lincoln School, there were only thirty-five kids in my class, and about six of those were the popular kids who did everything. But all at once, all six of them moved, and suddenly there was a void of popular people. Everyone was equal."

As elections for the following year's student-body officers approached, one of Sharlene's teachers pulled her aside and suggested, "Why don't you run for office?" "I was flabbergasted," Sharlene remembers, "and replied, 'Are you kidding? I'm not popular. I couldn't possibly win.'" Then the teacher asked, "Well, who else is going to win? Why don't you try?"

Trying meant doing things she'd never done before, things that didn't come naturally, such as giving campaign speeches and promoting herself. "I had to *force* myself to give those campaign speeches," Sharlene says, overemphasizing the words. "I was dead scared. It was not a pleasant experience for me to talk to people, period, let alone get up and talk in front of people." But something made her do it and do it competently, if not easily. As an eighth grader, she was elected student-body treasurer for the coming year.

"It was the first time I'd ever won anything in my life," Sharlene says excitedly, reliving the sensation of that first breakthrough. "And that opened it up for me, because suddenly I was one of the top four officers in student government. It just took me that one time to realize I was a lot more happy when I was involved."

During the following two years at the Lincoln School in Buenos Aires, Sharlene was elected to positions as student-body secretary, junior class president, and National Honor Society vice president. "I started to become more confident about myself, and I learned how to smile at people without feeling uncomfortable. That was a lot of it right there." In fact, she gained enough confidence to encourage her to compete in other areas. She quickly found that her tomboy inclinations went way beyond a casual interest in sports. As it turned out, she had a lot of raw, but natural, ability as well.

The instructor who coached all of the high school girls teams also supervised eighth grade girls P.E., and she regularly put her P.E. classes through full-fledged workouts. "We'd work on hurdles, the high jump, and so forth, just as though we were on the team," Sharlene remembers. "No matter how old we were or how good we were, we worked out on everything."

The more Sharlene practiced, the more she found that sports were in her blood. "I'd grown up with a soccer ball in my hands, but I didn't realize I was athletically coordinated until eighth grade." Her specialty? The 100-meter low hurdles. "All during my eighth grade year I worked on the hurdles, trying to get the three steps you have to have between each hurdle. I could get part of the way taking three

Sharlene took her love of track with her to Skyline High School in Salt Lake City, Utah

steps between each, but I could just not get it down for the length of the race."

Between her eighth and ninth grade years Sharlene grew an inch or so, and the first time she reported for practice as a ninth grader and took a run at the hurdles she managed to get in the required three steps, all the way down the track. She was elated and kept shouting, "I did it! I did it!"

Actually, she did much more than that. It wasn't long before she was breaking school records in the hurdles and even the high jump, which she never considered her specialty. But in Argentina there were very few, if any, dual track meets between rival schools, so Sharlene had only limited opportunity to find out how good she was until her tenth grade year. It was then that she and her teammates entered the Argentine national high school track meet—believed to be the largest high school meet in the world. Annually, some twenty thousand high school athletes gather in Buenos

Aires at the military academy to compete in the three-day event.

Sharlene was entered in the hurdles, high jump, and as anchor for the 4x100 relay team. From the beginning of her first major meet, things were exciting. When she reported in at the high jump preliminaries, her first event, she noticed that rather than the traditional thick styrofoam mats she'd been accustomed to landing on, only one thin mat was positioned in the pit where the high jumper was to land. "I took one look at that and knew there was no way they were going to get me over that bar if I had to land on that. I knew I'd break my back." A girl from the British school in Buenos Aires also voiced her concern, and together, they fussed until officials delayed the competition long enough to equip the pit with thick styrofoam padding. Sharlene and the girl from the British school were appeased, but dozens of other jumpers from the nine or ten high jump pits around the stadium had caught wind of what was taking place, and they too demanded the thick mats. It was not until several truck-loads of the foam pads were delivered inside the stadium that the high jump competition proceeded in earnest.

No sooner were things set for Sharlene's high jump competition to begin than her coach came running over. "Come on, you've got to be at the hurdles preliminaries right now." In order to allow Sharlene to compete at both ends, the high jump officials made a quick decision. "Why don't you take all of your qualifying jumps right now," they instructed her. And she did. "Everybody stood back and watched while I jumped from one height to the next," she says. "But I got so tired jumping one after the other that I didn't go very high." Not knowing how her performance would compare with the rest of the field, she dashed over to the track, where the hurdles were being run.

Some 140 girls were entered in the 100-meter hurdles. The preliminaries were scheduled for Friday, the semifinals

for Saturday, and the finals for Sunday. Sharlene won her
heat on Friday, which qualified her for the semifinals. "I'd no
sooner won that heat than my coach ran over and told me
I'd made the high jump finals, too, which stunned me, because high jump really wasn't my forte." Sharlene raced back
to the high jump finals, and out of two hundred girls entered
she took fifth place.

On Saturday, Sharlene won her semifinal heat in the
hurdles, which qualified her to race in the finals—on Sunday. Sharlene was the only individual on her team to reach
the finals in any event. And suddenly the thrill of victory
soured. "I'd told the coach beforehand that I couldn't compete on Sunday, but I don't think she'd let it sink in," Sharlene remembers of the experience. "She probably hadn't
considered the possibility of my making the finals. Needless
to say, she was very upset." The pressure progressed from
awkward to awful when the 4x100 relay team Sharlene an-
chored also reached the finals.

"Wouldn't you just ask your parents?" the coach prodded
Sharlene. "I'll talk to them for you. I'm sure they'd let you
make an exception and run this one time. You're the cap-
tain, you owe it to the team."

Sharlene shook her head, said she didn't need to ask her
parents, and that she couldn't, or wouldn't, run. What may
have seemed to be a complex decision for most talented
young athletes wasn't all that perplexing to Sharlene. "I'd
been taught that Sunday was a day for the Lord, and I had a
commitment there long before I had a commitment to the
track team. I didn't see any reason to ask my parents about
it. They'd always taught us that *we* knew what was right and
wrong and that we shouldn't have to be told all the time
what was right, that we needed to make our own decisions."

Sharlene didn't run. The relay team raced with a substitute anchor and lost. The girl who took first place in the
hurdles was the same girl Sharlene had beat in the semifinals

on Saturday. Sharlene admits, "It took the wind out of my sails. But if I had that gold, it would always remind me that I'd sold out and run on Sunday. And who knows, maybe if I'd rationalized and gone ahead and run, I would have fallen or tripped or something. I've always been superstitious about doing things that I knew really weren't right." (As an eight-year-old, she had stayed home sick from school one day, and her mother had warned her not to go outside. She went outside, fell on a large, rough boulder, and scarred her face. "Even now when my face is tan you can see the scar. It always reminds me that there are *always* consequences when you do something that you *know* you shouldn't.")

The following year, the Argentine nationals proved to be an instant replay. Again, at the outset, she told her coach she couldn't run on Sunday if she reached the finals. Again she competed. Again she reached the finals and did not run. Although it was annoying to never have her moment in the winner's circle, when evidence suggests she'd have been a walkaway winner, an even greater frustration was beginning to mount.

Not only was Sharlene "tall and leggy and fast," as her father puts it, but she also "swam well, ran well, and played most sports well. She was lean and muscular." She swam on the swim team, was a star on the school's volleyball team, and was a standout in about any sport she took a fancy to. She was also elected cheerleader her first year at Lincoln School, but after the boys made fun of her skinny legs, she lost interest and confined her energies to sports. In short, she was a natural athlete.

But as much as she loved them, sports weren't everything. Perhaps for the first time in her life, frustration began to build—not because she was on the outside straining to look in, but because there was not enough time to do everything.

There are those who think Sharlene could have been

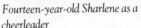
Fourteen-year-old Sharlene as a   *Practicing the harp in 1980*
cheerleader

an Olympic hurdler if she'd devoted herself strictly to that. "I think I could have done it," she says, referring to the Olympics, "because I have the long legs for it. I feel I had the speed, and I think I had the physical endurance and self-discipline to do it. But I was into too many things. I'd get up early to practice the piano before school, then stay after school for track, and then have to study and find time to practice the piano again in the afternoon."

Sharlene and her sisters Elayne and Janet rotated practicing shifts on the piano before and after school. "I'd get up at 5:30 or 5:15, and it would be my turn to play the piano from 6:00 to 6:30 in the morning. Then we all had to get in our practicing in the afternoon."

Piano wasn't the end of it. She wanted to learn to play the trumpet and took lessons from the high school band teacher. After a few months, she was playing second chair, and a short while later, first chair. She auditioned for the jazz band and made it. "Then there was the harp," Robert Wells remembers. "She wanted us to buy her a Paraguayan harp and give her harp lessons, and because she'd done so well on other instruments, we did. She's always been an intense practicer. Oh sure, there were plenty of times when she didn't practice enough on her own, but I'd say she suffered from less of that tendency than our other children."

Academics were also important to Sharlene, because academic competition in the Lincoln School was intense. She competed with students from other cultures who, in many instances, were accustomed to being measured against rigid and structured scholastic standards.

"The Japanese students were *incredible,* in mathematics especially," Sharlene says with confirmed admiration in her voice. "They were so disciplined. Some of my friends from India and Israel and other places were extremely advanced in science. We'd get together in study groups. I found that the United States is lackadaisical when it comes to discipline and challenge in school. Even though there were only thirty-five students in each grade, we had an average of two per class accepted to Harvard."

Academic competition was steep, in part because of the standard set by demanding instructors. Robert Wells explains that the American school, because it must lure instructors to Argentina and pay their way there, offers top dollar to attract top-flight professors, many of whom hold Ph.D.'s. "You've got tremendously qualified instructors who demand a high level of performance. After we returned to the United States our children told us it was much more difficult to get A's from the teachers at Lincoln School than from professors at local universities."

Sharlene believes at least a couple of her instructors had timely influence on her. Her chemistry teacher, called "Doc" by everyone, had taught chemistry at Harvard for ten years before moving to South America. "He was the type who'd pick on one student every day. If it was your day, he'd ask you every question the whole class period. And if you didn't know your stuff, you'd feel like a fool. So we *had* to study every day. He taught us to be conscientious about learning." Doc, who was German, always posted his favorite saying on the bulletin board: "Don't flirt with knowledge. Fall in love with knowledge." "I've tried to remember that ever since," Sharlene says.

"My world history teacher spoke eight languages fluently, and our math teacher taught us how to think on our own. He refused to explain everything to us. He'd say, 'It's explained in your book. Figure it out. Then if you can't figure it out, come back and we'll talk.' If we'd dare regurgitate answers on tests, he'd deduct points. My track coach helped, too. She couldn't be everywhere at once, so I had to work out on my own. She forced me to work hard and acquire some self-discipline." Sharlene was disciplined enough in high school to carry a 3.97 G.P.A.

Helen Wells says that's one quality her daughter had an early grasp on. "She's always been a goalsetter and a self-motivated person. When she was going to high school in Argentina, she'd read a scripture or an uplifting thought of some kind, write it on a card, and tape it above her bed on the wall or on her mirror or in the bathroom. Her room was cluttered with thoughts she could read every day. She'd also make a list of what she was going to wear each day for a week and tape it to the inside of her closet. Her sisters followed suit. And she started her own system of saving money. She'd have one jar for her tithing, another for her missionary fund, one for gifts, and a little one 'Just for Me.' She's always been disciplined."

In most areas, perhaps. Her father does point out at least one drawback, of sorts, that came from growing up in South America. "The kids grew up with maids who made the beds and did the dishes and served the table. None of our girls are the cookie-making type, though I suppose they *can* make cookies." Apart from the chores, servants may have introduced another element. "Maybe Sharlene waits to be waited on at times," he says. "But she does have a carryover of the aristocratic, maybe even spoiled, life. Now, she would undoubtedly think of that as an insult, and maybe I'm exaggerating things. I don't think she looks upon herself at all as being snobbish, and I don't think she is. I imagine there are people who see her that way. She does not think she's any better than anybody else, but she is used to having things done for her."

As might be expected, Sharlene doesn't see things that way. "Mom was always very careful about making sure we had responsibilities in the house. We've had chores ever since I can remember. I don't remember ever feeling, 'Oh, why can't somebody else do this?'" She does admit that living abroad presented her with unique opportunities at a relatively young age, which forced her to "grow up fast." Those experiences may have helped her gain a mature perspective of herself and the world, as well as acquire an air of apparent sophistication.

"In South America, I made friends from Egypt, Israel, Argentina, and New York," Sharlene explains. "Even though I haven't been many places, the world seems small to me. I had a good friend from Iran at the time of the hostage crisis, and though that was going on, it didn't stop us from being good friends. And there were friends from Egypt and Israel who got along fine. Sure, we discussed politics; it seemed that no matter what political or international issue we were discussing, there was someone who could speak from personal experience on the topic."

Her father feels that Sharlene's friendships in Buenos Aires allowed her to grow up, as she puts it, color-blind. "She didn't distinguish between nationalities and cultures and races. She learned to take people at face value, and that's a unique feature. Her sophistication comes from going to the opera, traveling throughout South America, meeting and socializing with people frequently, learning another language, and perhaps most of all, learning to love people from all over the world."

"I know there are differences between races and nationalities," Sharlene comments, "but I had the chance to learn to appreciate those differences and to not be afraid of them. Just because I'm different doesn't mean I'm any better than they are—or vice versa."

During the formative teenage years, when young people begin to determine how and where they'll fit into society, Sharlene did a turnaround, moving from feelings of inhibition to full and hectic participation in what life had to offer. She started slowly, testing the waters gradually when she arrived in Argentina. But in the course of a couple of years, she had plunged headfirst into the depths of involvement. "I often wonder what my life would have been like if we hadn't returned to South America," Sharlene says. "I don't think I would have ever come out of my shell if we'd stayed in the United States."

Despite the growth, she had her share of normal teenage problems. "Dad wouldn't let us wear makeup until we were sixteen, and I whined about that because I felt I was still homely. It bothered me." Sharlene laughs as she talks about this, evidently remembering the awkward moments. And, in fact, Sharlene Wells the teenager was a very average-looking girl. There was nothing to distinguish her physically from other girls, certainly nothing to indicate that she would become a beauty. The space between her front teeth didn't close entirely until the end of her junior year.

"Dad would say, 'You'll get pierced ears when you put a ring through your nose!' and I complained about that. I never had the money to dress in all the latest fashions. I just wore the basic cords, Oxford shirts and pullovers. And all the other girls had boyfriends. I was the *only girl* who never did. It got to be normal for me to be the one without a boyfriend, but it always bothered me that I was the one left out on that score."

Apart from her stubbornness, she had her share of shortcomings as well. Her mother says a major one was "a streak of jealousy. When she wanted to learn to play the harp, she didn't want her sisters to learn. She likes to set herself apart; she likes being distinctive. And she wants to be number one. If she isn't, she doesn't crumble, but she always works to be at the top of the heap."

Robert Wells summarizes, "Charlie started to develop that endearing combination of being an attractive girl who was also very competitive, loved sports, and went at everything with enthusiasm. She'd beat any boy she could at anything, still does. But even though she was athletic and more coordinated than many others I've seen, she suffered through adolescence like everyone else. She suffered through feeling awkward and ungainly. She suffered through pimples and from unrequited love. She stumbled, she failed. There were tears and uncertainties. We never thought we had a Miss America on our hands."

Chapter 5

Strong Family and Religious Ties

It was only a few days before Lincoln High School's Southern Star Ball, the annual Christmas dance and argually the biggest event of the school year. The grapevine had gotten word to Sharlene that David, the most popular guy in school, was going to ask *her* to the ball. The news would have thrilled Sharlene had it not been for one problem. She was fifteen-going-on-sixteen, in three months. That night Sharlene gingerly broached the subject.

"Mom, I think David's going to ask me to the dance."

"How do you feel about that, Sharlene?"

She replied slowly, "I guess I've already decided what I'm going to tell him, but if he asks, it sure is going to be hard to say no."

"Sharlene, you know you can make your own decision on this."

There was a long pause. Sharlene finally answered, "I know that."

David did ask her to the dance. Sharlene told him thanks but maybe another time—in fact, any time in three months. The result? David didn't go to the ball either.

"I don't remember Mom and Dad lecturing about what we could or couldn't do," Sharlene says. "But I do remember my dad saying over and over again, 'We have a Wells family standard.' He didn't put it in Church or religious terms. We always knew the Church standards, but we didn't stick to the rules just because of the Church, but also because of what was expected in our family. I grew up thinking it was as important to behave myself because of our family standard as the Church standards. We couldn't, for example, date until we were sixteen. We didn't watch television on Sunday, unless something extraordinary was on like *The Ten Commandments*. We didn't drink Cokes."

There were other family standards. Curfew was a big one, and Helen Wells had her own way of monitoring the situation. "We always had to tell our parents where we were going and when we'd be back, or we were in big trouble," Sharlene emphasizes. "If I'd ask Mom for permission to go to a dance or something, she'd say, 'Okay, but I want you back here at five minutes before eleven o'clock.' I'd think, 'What's the big deal with the five minutes?' When I'd come walking in at eleven o'clock, Mom would be really disappointed with me." A discussion would ensue in which Sharlene would again ask what difference five minutes could possibly make. Her mother would reply, "It's the fact that I asked you to be home five minutes ago, and you were not."

"Sometimes it takes me a little while to catch on," Sharlene admits, "but after a while I realized she was serious. So if she said she wanted me home by midnight, I'd get there five minutes before. The next time I asked to go somewhere, she'd let me stay out later. She never said that's what she'd do, but I gradually learned that the more trustworthy I became, the more responsibility and freedom she gave me."

Robert Wells says that in her teenage years Sharlene was "willing to obey family standards and the Church standards: not dating until she was sixteen, not staying out late, calling us when she was going to be late. She was readily obedient and maybe a little easier to handle than some of the other kids." Helen Wells says simply, "I hope she learned from our example, but really it just seemed easy for her to internalize good values. Her sense of right and wrong is very clear and always has been."

Sharlene (left) with sister Elayne celebrating Christmas at a lake in Bariloche, Argentina, 1978

Though she wasn't overbearing about pressing her values and opinions on others, Sharlene wasn't shy about making them known either. It seemed that her unique high school experience set the stage for a number of interactions.

Robert Wells explains that although Sharlene tracted with some of the lady missionaries at times, her favorite missionary activities evolved more naturally. "Some of her best friends were what they called M.K.'s, or missionary kids—the children of missionaries of other denominations. She became used to discussing points of doctrine in a 'This is what I believe, what do you believe?' type of interchange. She respects other religions and individuals who also go out and sacrifice to serve the Lord."

"Most of my friends in South America smoked or drank or did things I didn't agree with," Sharlene says, "but it didn't bother me. Just because I disagreed with their actions didn't mean I didn't like them as people. If some of them took drugs or something like that, I'd use the 'Come on, you don't need that stuff' approach. You've got to be friends with people and accept them for who they are first, and then try to help them. It's the light touch. What did Christ do? He didn't work with the righteous; he worked with the sinners."

By and large, Sharlene practiced what she preaches, taking a low-key approach to sharing the gospel. From several reports, by the time she left South America many of her friends had abandoned cigarettes and alcohol. Any influence she had came from the subtle impact of example rather than out-and-out proselytizing.

As a student-body officer at Lincoln High School, Sharlene took her turn working the concession stand at athletic events. On one occasion during her sophomore year she asked the faculty advisor why Coca Cola was the only soft drink sold. "Because nobody would buy anything else," was the answer. Sharlene pled a case for giving something else a trial run—like Fanta orange. The advisor relented, and the very first night of the experiment the Fanta sold out before the Coke.

Sharlene came by her nerve in several ways. She thrived in the mission field environment and traveled frequently with her parents to zone conferences and on other assignments where her father would call on Sharlene and her sisters to extemporaneously bear their testimonies and sing. "When he'd do that, we'd always exclaim, 'Oh, Dad!' but really we loved it. The mission tours were terrific. There was nothing more thrilling than being in the midst of those missionaries with their white shirts on and singing all those songs."

On those tours of one zone conference after another, there would often be as many as three or four meetings a day. Even though her two sisters Elayne and Janet (by this time the older children were attending school in the States)

Practicing the guitar at home in Argentina

would often stay in the hotel room during the conferences, Sharlene would insist on going with her parents. Helen remembers Sharlene accompanying them to the conferences. "She would troop with us to meeting after meeting and take copious notes, most of which were in Spanish. She seemed to thrive on it."

At Christmastime, the family would accompany Elder Wells on his trips to Bariloche in southern Argentina, a beautiful resort area that Sharlene describes as being a cross between the Swiss Alps, the Grand Tetons, and Lake Tahoe. "It's gorgeous," she says excitedly. "There is a lot of European culture in Argentina, and this particular village is of Swiss architecture."

The Wellses would typically hold a poetry-writing contest among their daughters. The object was to describe their surroundings and experiences, and the winner usually received a modest prize—ten thousand to twenty thousand pesos. "We'd stay at a chalet on top of a beautiful green hill with a lake below. On Christmas morning, we'd spend time with the missionaries. Then they'd all come to Christmas dinner, and we'd have spaghetti. Can you believe that? I felt as though I was actually out in the field with the missionaries. Ever since I was ten I've wanted to go on a mission," she adds, "but that just sparked my interest."

Her mission field upbringing and tendency toward obedience notwithstanding, Sharlene had an obstinate streak in her. Her father says she's stubborn and headstrong. "In other words, she can be righteously indignant. She is very stubborn when sticking up for her own rights, and she does not back down."

Helen Wells confirms that. "Sharlene has a mind of her own. In her early teenage years, she was always open to my suggestions, but later on she'd learned a little too much to always listen to me. So there was, and still is, quite a little bantering back and forth between us. She's strong willed and rarely changes her mind. During her high school years, I started getting the feeling that she knew a lot more than I did, and I say that tongue in cheek."

Though she might be headstrong, Sharlene says she is not hot tempered. "I've never been an emotional person. I can count on one hand the times I've cried tears. I rarely get mad and fly off the handle." Almost everyone who knows her confirms this as fact. However, she will admit to losing her cool a few times when "her personal character was being attacked."

One example of this occurred at Lincoln High School after Sharlene made the swim team. At a three-day meet for the province championships (similar to a state championship meet) she reached the finals in the backstroke, which were to be held on Sunday. "All week long people had been badgering me about swimming on Sunday. My teammates, the coach, everyone kept saying things like, 'Oh, come on

Sharlene (second from left) as a student-body officer

Sharlene, ask your parents,' or 'It's ridiculous that you won't swim on Sunday.' One afternoon, I was sitting near the pool and one girl who thought she ran the school came up and lit into me again. I got so upset that I turned around and let her have it! When I do get mad, I talk very, very fast. I told her in no uncertain terms that I respected her beliefs, and it was about time she learned to respect mine!"

During her five years in South America, Sharlene acquired strong feelings for several things—principally the gospel and her parents, the two of which became inseparably intertwined. As Sharlene explains, "In the mission field, we were constantly in defense of the Church. There were always questions being asked about why we did this or that, so I bore my testimony often. I wish everyone had the opportunity to live in the mission field. That's where my testimony really grew.

"At the same time, I drew very close to my family. There are many young people today who've grown up with their best friends becoming even more important to them than their parents. But we'd move up to the United States, then down to South America, then back up again, and my friends would come and go. My only roots were in the family. High school is such an impressionable time, and that's when I was learning and becoming who I am. I guess who and what I am has almost totally to do with my family and the gospel."

Chapter 6

All Good Things Must End

Whoever said that all good things must end was a spoil-sport. Unfortunately, that person was also right. At the end of 1980, Elder Wells's assignment changed, and he and the family returned to Salt Lake City. Sharlene wasn't thrilled about the move, though it didn't send her into a tailspin either. She was almost seventeen and in the middle of her junior year. She had already begun anticipating the time when she'd return to the States to attend college, most likely at Brigham Young University. Nevertheless, there was the challenge of once again making a go of it in an environment that she remembered as being less than hospitable.

One of the first things she asked her brother-in-law Grant Pace was, "Do they date up here?" When he replied yes, that dating was still a popular institution in the States, she got right to the point. "Do you think anybody will ask me out?" "Trust me," he answered, "in a couple of weeks you'll be dating."

Unfortunately, the transition wasn't quite that smooth. "Charlie felt ostracized when we moved back to Salt Lake," Robert Wells says with candor. "Coming into the cliquish high school groups here, she felt left out. And, once again, that was foreign to her, because the Latin environment is much warmer. Almost everybody was friendly down there. Of course, her school was smaller there, and sometimes in smaller schools you avoid these kinds of problems."

In part, Sharlene's timing was unfortunate. She was a

Family portrait in 1982. Back row: Elayne, David, Janet;
front row: Elder Wells, Sharlene, Sister Wells

second-semester junior when she entered Skyline High
School in Salt Lake City. Social groups within her class were
already tightly defined. In addition, as the new kid on the
block, she found an unenthusiastic response from classmates
when she very quickly stepped in line for highly sought-after
kudos and recognitions.

Assuming that high school life at Skyline would be similar to what she'd experienced in Buenos Aires, Sharlene
plunged with predictable energy into as much as she could
handle. She auditioned for madrigals and was selected for
the group. She sang in concert choir, was named president
of the local chapter of the National Honor Society, spent
at least two hours practicing the piano daily, took her first
voice lessons (at one time from Tabernacle Choir soloist
JoAnn Ottley), and ran track until a slight knee injury kept
her out of competitive athletics her senior year. To stay in

shape and quench her thirst for physical activity, she took up a number of what she calls leisure sports—rappeling, hiking, and racquetball became favorites.

Sharlene's tendency to dabble in a variety of activities, with at least moderate success, rubbed some of her peers the wrong way. Classmates were annoyed by this upstart, who'd spent most of her years outside the United States, stepping in line for accolades that might have gone their way. When, at the end of her junior year, she was chosen a member of the seminary council for the following year, peers and parents cried foul.

"I guess you can't blame the parents of sons and daughters who'd grown up through the school system," Helen Wells says. "This new girl moves in and within three months is asked to sit on the seminary council." But the episode stunned Sharlene. "I was a confident person," she explains, "and had held leadership positions in the Church and school in South America. I assumed I'd been asked to be a part of the council because I was capable and could make a contribution, but lots of parents were upset. They felt I'd been selected because I was the daughter of a General Authority, and that hurt. I'd never faced that kind of criticism before."

By and large, Sharlene took it on the chin. As her father puts it, "She's always been a fun-loving, happy person. She doesn't let a lot get her down, and she doesn't stay discouraged very long." In the meantime, she continued to dive into everything she could manage. "In South America people would say to me, 'But you're trying to do everything,' and I just thought that everybody did everything. I didn't think much of it because I was in a small school where there were lots of opportunities. Then, when we moved back to the United States, I still wanted to do as much as I could. That's just the way I'd grown up."

At the end of her junior year, Sharlene received yet

another recognition when she was selected as one of three delegates from Skyline High School to Girls' State. This opportunity was to prove fortuitous.

At Girls' State, it was traditional for the state director of the Junior Miss pageant to be given the opportunity to inform the large audience of senior girls about the Junior Miss pageant, a contest restricted to seniors. During Sharlene's week at Girls' State, the Junior Miss presentation was once again outlined and promoted. In the process, she found that this program was structured to evaluate girls on five points: talent, scholarship, physical fitness, poise and appearance, and interview.

Even so, at first, Sharlene was unimpressed. "I was always the one who said, 'You'll never get me into one of those contests.' I had always thought beauty pageants were made up of a bunch of airheads, and that all they did was wander around onstage. I thought that was wimpy." But when Sharlene found out that the Junior Miss pageant was not a beauty pageant (there is no swimsuit competition), and that handsome sums of scholarship money were available to the winners, she became more interested in the idea. In fact, her appetite was whetted.

"When I was a banker with Citibank," Robert Wells says, "the kids took it for granted that I would provide their education for them, which I would have been very happy to do. But as a General Authority, I don't enjoy that kind of income. I told them all they would have to pay for their own education. Sharlene saw the Junior Miss pageant and its scholarship money as a way to do that."

Sharlene returned from Girls' State with a suitcase full of Junior Miss literature, and right away she asked her mother what she thought about it. "I thought it looked like a lot of work," Helen admits, "but I decided that if Sharlene really wanted to try it, we ought to help her." With her mother's consent, Sharlene entered the local pageant, but was skeptical about her chances. "In the back of my mind, I still had the misconception that this was a beauty contest, and I was being judged on my face and figure. I kept thinking, 'There is no way I'm going to get anywhere in this.'"

Because there is no local pageant for girls in Salt Lake City, those selected by a group of judges go straight to the state competition. Sharlene was chosen to compete in the state pageant and subsequently won the title of Utah's Junior Miss. Despite the title, she wondered if it hadn't all been a fluke. She couldn't believe she had qualified to compete in the national Junior Miss pageant in Mobile, Alabama. While at the national pageant, she gained a new perspective. "I had finally decided I looked okay. Back at the Junior Miss nationals, the girls were not the gorgeous type. It was a group of cute but not wowy all-American girls." She didn't win the national title, but her performance on the Paraguayan harp was good enough to clinch the overall talent award, which carried a six-thousand-dollar scholarship prize. When the dust had settled, Sharlene's Junior Miss experience had satisfied her original goal, netting her nearly eight thousand dollars in scholarship money—more than enough to pay for music lessons, books, and college tuition.

With her Junior Miss success, Sharlene started to attract attention from peers and well-wishers. This compensated only in part for the fact that her brother-in-law's prediction concerning dating had proven optimistic. To say the least, Sharlene had not been besieged by requests for dates. "Sharlene could probably count on one hand the number of fellows who asked her out during her year and a half at Skyline. But that didn't bother me," Helen Wells adds, wryly. Although it did not bother her mother, it bothered Sharlene. "I've never been a socialite, or really wanted to date a lot. But I've never turned down lots of dates either. To tell the truth, I've just never had lots of offers."

There are probably logical reasons for that. One might

At the Junior Miss pageant in Mobile, Alabama, with Michael Landon

have been the intimidation factor, though Sharlene still has trouble swallowing that explanation. As she points out, her high school yearbooks and photo albums prove that as a teenager her appearance was nothing out of the ordinary. Pigtails, the gap between her teeth, and her tomboyish image were on the opposite end of the glamour spectrum. "Nobody ever told me that I was even cute back in those days. I guess a lot of girls get told, but I never did."

It could be that her high G.P.A. and position as president of the National Honor Society shooed some suitors off. In Argentina, her standards and membership in the Church undoubtedly kept the non-LDS fellows at arm's length. Regardless, unanswered questions ran through her mind at frequent intervals. "I wasn't running into the normal situations

Sharlene with her date to homecoming at Skyline High,
Devon O'Brien

that all my friends were," she explains. "They were all saying, 'Oh, this guy tried to get out of hand last night,' and I
was thinking to myself, 'Nobody ever tried to get out of hand
with me. I must not be much to look at.'"

Several years later, she ran into a German friend she'd
gone to school with in South America, and he told her,
"You know why you didn't get asked out much down there?
Because you were so intimidating. Your religion set you
apart, and all the guys knew you wouldn't do certain things.
The second reason is that you were so good looking." "What?"
Sharlene exclaimed in response. "No one ever told me."

There was an additional intimidating factor. Once back in the States, Sharlene persisted in talking about her experiences in South America, and that put some peers off. Helen Wells remembers hearing a grapevine report that one young man who dated Sharlene later remarked, "All she does is talk about Sharlene, Sharlene, and Sharlene."

"I talked to her about it, because I wanted her to refine those kinds of things," Helen says. "She has never been a cocky person—reserved maybe, but never cocky. But to those in her new high school who didn't know her, she may have come across that way. She's always been so enthusiastic about all of her experiences and interests, which have run the gamut, that it's been hard for her to contain herself. That may have contributed to the uphill battle with friends that she encountered in Salt Lake City."

During Sharlene's last eighteen months of high school her personality and character developed even further. In a short five years, she'd moved from one end of the spectrum to the other. She grew from a very self-conscious, shy, uncertain girl to a multifaceted, multitalented young woman who was determined to get things done and to do them well. When she found herself frustrated at being intrigued with so many things, her voice teacher, JoAnn Ottley, gave her some timely counsel. She told Sharlene that one day she'd be able to narrow her interests and concentrate on a *few* areas. In the meantime, it was a blessing to have diversified goals to work toward. Sharlene took the advice to heart. "Other people have told Mom and Dad that we're a family of achievers. I don't think any of us have ever looked at it that way. It's not as though we've ever sat down in Family Home Evening and been told to achieve certain things. We just all started working together down in South America. And Mom and Dad have always set the example, that we should always do the best we can do."

Chapter 7

The Quiet Life?

How does the old saying go, about paving roads with good intentions? When Sharlene entered BYU as a freshman, she had a raft of well-intentioned objectives. "I was so sick of being involved in everything under the sun that I wasn't going to do anything but concentrate on academics, practice the piano, and take voice lessons."

In fairness, Sharlene did make an effort to slow down. But looking for something that would challenge her academically, she signed up for an upper division honors class. Then, she'd barely had chance to unpack her bags when the bishop of her student ward called her to serve as Relief Society president. "It was overwhelming," she admits. "I'd never even been to Relief Society. I had no idea what a Relief Society president was supposed to do. At least I had some speaking and leadership experience to draw on, and that helped. But ward leaders were expected to attend all the social gatherings and activities, and I was trying to cut back on that kind of thing. Now that I look back at it, I don't feel I did all that I could have in that position. I'll know better if there's ever a next time."

As the year progressed, Sharlene's resolution to slow down gradually went down the drain. She worked on campaigns for student-body officers and played on the coed volleyball team that took second in the entire campus tournament ("The only reason we didn't win was that we played all season with only five players, though we were supposed to have six. In the championship game, six people showed up, and it messed up our whole strategy!"). She also began to make some good friends, among them Janice Spendlove and Robyn Thompson.

Robyn remembers her first impression of Sharlene. "She was intimidating. Here was this gorgeous, tan blonde who I thought had to be from California. I'd see her singing around the piano in the dorm with a group of guys. Then I found out that her dad was a General Authority, and I thought she was untouchable. It seemed as though she was perfect."

The following year Sharlene and Robyn lived in the same apartment. "Sharlene wasn't perfect after all," Robyn says, "but if I could say one thing about her, it would be that she is a good friend. I guess that's because she is a genuinely good person. I remember one morning when I was having a bad day and Charlie was in a rush to get off to class. A few minutes after she'd left, the door opened, and she walked back in. When I asked her what she'd forgotten she said,

Sharlene with friends at BYU. Back row: Sharlene, Heather Ebeling, Janice Spendlove; bottom row: Robyn Thompson

'Oh, I just thought you needed a hug.' That was that, and she was gone again. She's the kind of person who'll be there for you when you need her."

Toward the end of her freshman year, at Robyn's prompting, Sharlene decided to try out for Young Ambassadors, BYU's highly acclaimed and widely traveled collegiate variety show. "I'd always wanted to be in Young Ambassadors," Sharlene explains. "But at that point I'd never sung with a microphone, and never done any solo work. Plus, I could not dance." She laughs, apparently calling to mind images of her few attempts on the dance floor. "I figured I'd chalk this one up to experience."

Sharlene and some eight or nine hundred other talented hopefuls showed up for tryouts that spring. Everyone had to be videotaped while singing a ballad and an up-tempo number. "I'd never even held a mike," Sharlene says, "but I just sang my heart out. I thought I'd blown it. As a matter of fact, I didn't even check the callback list. My roommate got in touch with me and told me I'd made callback. I asked if she knew what I had to do next, and she said, 'I think it's the dance auditions.' I started laughing and thought to myself, 'I wonder how far I can carry this on?'"

Sharlene hurried back to auditions. Randy Boothe, the director of Young Ambassadors, vividly remembers just how well she performed in the dance tryout. "In the dance audition, Sharlene looked like a woman basketball player—just kind of tall and lanky. You could tell she had *never* been on a dance floor before. In fact, when she showed up to the dance auditions she was wearing a dress, and we had to send her out with a couple of kids who'd taken a lot of dance to see if they could find something she could wear. She borrowed a pair of tennis shoes from one girl, a pair of sweat pants from somebody else, and a T-shirt from someone else. That's how she did her first dance audition."

Sharlene hasn't forgotten the scenario, either. "There I

was, wearing all this borrowed stuff. Everyone else looked like they were straight out of *Fame*, and I looked like I'd come right out of *Rocky III*. It was embarrassing." She laughs about it now. At the time, it wasn't nearly as humorous. "Even though I really wanted to be in Young Ambassadors, I knew there was no chance, so I wasn't taking it seriously. The one thought that kept running through my mind was that all I could do was rely on my personality and just smile. They would teach us the dance routine, and then call up three at a time to repeat it. The first time I got called up there, with tons of people watching, I forgot the whole thing. So I just stood and smiled, but I was thinking to my-self, 'They must be getting a hoot out of this.'"

After the dance audition, Sharlene instinctively went to get her things to leave, feeling certain tryouts were over, for her at least. That's when she was told she'd made the first dance cut. "I couldn't believe it," she says, with some amaze-ment in her voice, "because I knew I shouldn't have even made the first voice cut, let alone the dance cut. At that point I started wondering if there was a purpose in all this, and I started getting the feeling that I might make it."

Why, amid such fierce competition, did she get that far? Randy Boothe explains. "There was no question that she was confident. I'll never forget that day when she came strid-ing in, wearing a beautiful white layered dress. She was *so* confident and made everyone feel *so* comfortable. You see, not only are we looking for talent, but we're looking for people who will be able to make friends for the university and the Church worldwide. She seemed to have the ability to come in and make everyone feel immediately comfort-able. It was also obvious that she was a natural onstage. This is going to sound funny at this point, but we often get the beauty-queen-type girls trying out, the ones who walk in with their make-up on and hair all foofed up, as though they're about to walk onstage in some major pageant. There's nothing wrong with that, but those girls give us a plastic exterior look. Sharlene, on the other hand, walked in just as unassuming and natural as if she'd barely run off the track."

Sharlene was one of thirty-two (sixteen men, sixteen women) who were selected to make up the two performance troupes of the Young Ambassadors. From that point on, all hope of staying uninvolved was gone. Young Ambassadors was a jealous taskmaster. In a matter of days, Sharlene had been given her first solo parts. They weren't big, but were much more than she had expected. She'd never considered herself a soloist, but Randy Boothe helped boost her confidence, explaining that her low, throaty voice had appealing qualities. "Sharlene doesn't have a big range," Randy says, "but she's got a magnificent low range. In those terms, she's done a lot with what she's got." But experience has its price.

Sharlene didn't realize how much time Y.A. was going to take. "There were two weeks of intensive all-day rehearsals before school began in the fall. Then, after school started, we'd have a 3:00 dance class, then maybe a 5:00 rehearsal for the show. At 7:00, I'd go study until 9:00, then I'd run and get something else done. It was grueling. Plus, it killed my social life, which I didn't have much of anyway. My whole life was Young Ambassadors."

"I don't think Sharlene had any idea what she was getting into," Randy Boothe comments, "both from a talent standpoint and the standpoint of the time commitment that would be involved to get her dance up to the level that we could use her choreographically onstage. I know she was torn in the beginning months because she was such an excellent student and was used to spending her off time either studying or dating—particularly playing tennis or racquetball with every guy on the block, and usually beating them."

There were times when Sharlene seriously questioned

The Young Ambassadors at Niagara Falls during a tour

her involvement with Young Ambassadors. She worried about her grades and about the huge blocks of time Y.A. demanded. And when, after the first semester, her G.P.A. dropped to 3.6, she wondered if her days with Y.A. weren't numbered. That's when she began to realize there was more to Young Ambassadors than prestige and the thrill of being onstage, and she began to find it easier to justify the time involved. Randy explains further, "By the time we started going on tour, Sharlene had caught the vision of what a public relations and missionary tool Young Ambassadors really is. She blossoms in any situation like that.

"She *loves* to express herself, to communicate with people. We'd go to a hospital or convalescent home and somebody would have her cornered within two or three minutes. I can't think of a Young Ambassador who's placed more Book of Mormons in the history of the group. She was always sharing an incredible number of Book of Mormons

Sharlene and friend Leanne Lee visit a lighthouse in Maine during a Young Ambassador tour

with people who sincerely seemed to want them because of a conversation they'd had with her."

Because she was a natural at public relations, Randy Boothe named Sharlene the student P.R. leader. Subsequently, she handled television and radio interviews and radio talk shows for the group while they were on tour. Randy remembers Sharlene coaching her peers in media savvy. "When we were on the bus on tour, she'd ask the kids questions about the university and the Church, and have them respond so they'd be practiced when they had to be interviewed by members of the media."

Sharlene also proved to be a natural onstage. "She's a ham to the max," Randy claims. "The audiences really got with her because she loved what she was doing, and it was obvious. I think that would probably describe her approach to life in general. She loves it." Whether dressed as a clown for a circus number or country/western style for a hoedown, she was a crowd-pleaser.

Each year the Young Ambassadors, who collectively have been around the world dozens of times, take at least one major tour. They've traveled to nearly every continent. During Sharlene's first year with the group, their tour took them across the United States, from Utah to Boston and back. Randy believes it proved to be a valuable training ground. "That tour was draining. In one location, for example, in Waukegan, Illinois, north of Chicago, we did seven performances in one day. That takes a certain amount of positive mental attitude because it was a killer show in terms of output. Sharlene and the other kids handled it so well. I think that's a quality and an experience that served her well when she became Miss America and had to take on a grueling schedule."

Specifically, she was exposed to the demands of constant travel and the pressure of repeat performances. But it doesn't appear that the pace "interfered" with her life-style or personality much. "Invariably," Randy says, "after we finished dinner, usually provided by the host ward or stake and served in the Relief Society room, and sang a thank you to those who'd prepared the meal, Sharlene was right into the cultural hall with a basketball, ready to play a quick game with the fellows.

"And, one aside, she eats like a horse. I've never seen a girl who could put away more at McDonald's than Sharlene. At one point, towards the end of the tour, we were getting concerned because she was starting to develop a little bread-basket. About that time, we were eating at this one restaurant, and she turned to me—completely serious—and said, 'Which one do you think has the least calories, chocolate cake or chocolate pudding?'"

In a word, Randy Boothe describes Sharlene as spontaneous. "You can't predict what she's going to say or how she's going to react in a situation, because she's her own woman, which I find refreshing for a young woman in the Church. In that respect she's a role model, because she thinks deeply, studies things out carefully to form her own opinion, and then expresses herself openly and honestly."

The hectic United States tour produced dozens of memorable moments, perhaps none of which was more powerful and yet serene than one rare morning when, free from the pressure of performing, the Young Ambassadors visited the Sacred Grove outside Palmyra, New York. "A light rain had just fallen," Sharlene recalls, "and we were given a few minutes to be to ourselves. When I walked into that area, my first instinct was to look up through the trees as Joseph Smith would have done. But at the same time, I wanted to look down. It was such a humbling yet a thrilling experience to be right there.

"I've never been an emotional person. Things are more factual to me. But I knew when I was standing there that our Father in Heaven lives, and that Jesus Christ came with him to visit Joseph at that spot. It was so clear to me. It wasn't as though I was feeling, 'Oh, I hope they did, because that's what I believe.' I knew it was true. And it doesn't hit me that way all the time. When you get caught up in the things that go on every day, it's easy to forget how real this life and the gospel are, and what we're really here for. But I will never forget the feeling I had that day."

The influence on Sharlene of that and other Young Ambassador experiences was powerful enough to persuade her to reaudition for the following year's troupe. She did, and was invited to return. Sharlene minces no words about the effect Young Ambassadors had on her during her sophomore year at BYU. "It was an essential experience, considering what lay ahead of me. Young Ambassadors taught me how to sing and perform in front of people, how to ad lib in front of a

Sharlene preparing for time alone in the Sacred Grove

crowd. I'd never been on camera before, I'd never been interviewed on radio or television. I'd never had or worked closely with good friends, and I'd never had as much confidence in my talents. I'm sure I would never have been named Miss America if it weren't for Y.A."

Chapter 8

The Run for Miss Utah

After Sharlene faired so well in Junior Miss competition, it was inevitable that interested friends and observers would encourage her to run for Miss Utah. Sharlene admits she was flattered by the attention, but her initial response was a blunt, "Come on, that's a beauty contest. I couldn't even get into that one."

Those who knew her well had anticipated her hesitations and were prepared with convincing arguments. Did Sharlene realize that the Miss America pageant system was the largest scholarship foundation for women in the world; that a full fifty percent of the judges' score was based on talent; that in Utah the swimsuit competition was held in private; and that, in fact, the Miss America national committee chafes at the term *beauty pageant* and at the notion that the mammoth system exploits young women? (Albert Marks, chairman of the Miss America pageant, told *USA Today*, "Any organization that provides $4.2 million annually in scholarship money . . . and that provides opportunity for some eighty thousand young women a year, can hardly be called exploitive. It's been said by some that if one were to use the word *exploit*, the shoe would be on the other foot. It is the young women who exploit the Miss America pageant, and we solicit that." [14 September 1984.])

Having lived most of her teenage life in South America, Sharlene had never even seen a Miss America pageant or attended a local pageant. But her friend who'd been involved in pageants in her home state of Kansas, Robyn Thompson, pressed the issue. She insisted that Sharlene was a shoo-in as Miss Utah. Intrigued about the possibilities of adding to her scholarship fund, Sharlene casually mentioned to her mother that it might be worth a try, and agreed to at least attend a meeting for girls interested in running for Miss Salt Lake Valley.

She vividly remembers the occasion. "There were nine other girls there, and they all had their bouffant hair and were all dolled up. I thought, 'Oh brother, what am I getting myself into?'" But after she got better acquainted with the girls and found them to be intelligent, talented, and as uncertain as she was, she decided to give it a go.

"I didn't place much importance on it at first," Sharlene's mother confesses. So little, in fact, that she almost failed to pick up the Miss Salt Lake Valley application in time. "We got her a dress at the last minute, she worked a little to polish a number on the harp, and that was about all there was to that first try."

Sharlene won the title of Miss Salt Lake Valley, which automatically qualified her to compete in the Miss Utah pageant. "I was sure I'd won because of my talent, which had always been my forte," Sharlene says. "I also knew my interview had been strong. But when it came to the swimsuit competition, I thought they were laughing me out of the auditorium."

She entered the Miss Utah pageant with the same attitude. Again, she and her parents went to almost no expense in preparing for the event. Sharlene used the same gown she'd worn in the Miss Salt Lake Valley pageant, wore a Chilean outfit her mother had brought home from Chile, which Helen Wells admits "wasn't the best," for her talent competition, and borrowed a suit to wear for the interview. Helen Wells (who was with daughter Elayne at the Junior Miss nationals—Sharlene had passed the state title on to her

younger sister) wasn't able to attend the pageant, so Robert
Wells provided moral support. It was at that pageant that he
first seriously took notice of his daughter's performance.

"I'd never thought of Sharlene as a beauty. But when
she competed for Miss Utah that first year, I began to recognize that she had a very graceful, queenly walk. I could start
to see the transformation." He could also see that she was
noticeably weak in some areas. "The moment I saw the
other girls come out in their fancy, sequined, thousand-
dollar dresses, I could tell that the hundred-dollar chiffon
wasn't going to cut it. After I saw the other girls perform, I
realized that Sharlene's harp, though unique, didn't allow
her to communicate with the judges. And, I could see that
she was kind of skinny, maybe too skinny. So I could tell
from almost the beginning that she wouldn't win."

She didn't win, but at age nineteen, she was the second
runner up. As it turned out, Sharlene's strong showing in
that first Miss Utah pageant was a significant turning point.
She started taking herself and her chances more seriously.
Her parents did likewise, and others took note.

As early as Wednesday of pageant week, Rebecca
Simpson, cochairman responsible for securing Miss Utah
pageant judges, had noticed Sharlene. Because of her official
capacity, she was not allowed to interact with the contestants, but that did not keep her from making a judgment.
"The first time I saw Sharlene was during her interview that
year. She walked into the room, sat down in front of five
judges, and turned what was to be an interview into a conversation. I could tell that this was a girl with unlimited potential. You could sense it. Here was a girl who could think
out loud and express herself, even at that age. I told my husband that that girl would be the next Miss Utah."

Kenn Barry, director of the New York state pageant and
a man who's been involved with the Miss America program
for well over twenty years, was one of the judges that year.

Afterwards he told Sharlene that she needed another year of experience and maturity, but encouraged her to try again the following year. His parting remark seemed outlandish. "I see you as the next Miss America."

"After that pageant, the judges told us what Sharlene needed," Robert Wells says. "They said she needed some clothes, and she needed to do something with her talent number so she could interact with the judges better." Photographers started remarking that Sharlene was going to be a beauty, and some of their pictures began to show what happened when they understood her face. "I began to see that Sharlene was becoming an unusually graceful and beautiful girl," her father adds, "so I told her that if she wanted to try again the following year, I'd be willing to invest some money in the project."

Sharlene and her mother immediately began to plan her wardrobe for a second stab at Miss Utah. As early as September they contacted Salt Lake City dressmaker Penelope Mackay and described the gown they had in mind as well as an outfit to wear for the talent competition. The gown Sharlene wanted was to be a deep aqua graduating to a light shade at the top, and was to be made entirely of reembroidered French lace and adorned with rhinestones and thousands of tiny, tube-like bugle beads.

The dressmaker designed and made the dress, but in the interest of frugality suggested that Helen Wells do the beading. "I wish I'd kept a time card," Helen says of the project. "It was incredibly time-consuming. I still can't believe I ever got it done." In fact, everyone got into the act. "A couple of nights when Bob was home, I showed him how to string the beads, and he helped me that way." Robert Wells says, "When we were done we'd turned a three hundred dollar dress into a thousand dollar gown." But fancy dress and all, the next year she almost didn't get to compete.

Early in her sophomore year at BYU, thinking that the

Helen Wells sewing the beads on Sharlene's dress, with a little help from Elder Wells

Miss BYU competition was a franchise for the Miss Utah pageant, Sharlene entered. "That was a killer," she remembers, "running for Miss BYU while being in Young Ambassadors." Y.A. rehearsals went until 6:00 every night. During pageant week, Sharlene had to be at the pageant by no later than 7:30. "That meant running home, showering, doing my hair, running back and being in place—not to mention finding time to polish my talent number." She was the first person to attempt both Young Ambassadors and Miss BYU at the same time. She did it primarily because she assumed that, if she won, she'd qualify once again for the Miss Utah pageant.

Again, there was very little expense involved. At that point Sharlene's designer gown was still in the planning stages, so she borrowed a dress for the competition. Her family didn't do much more than drive down to see her perform.

She won.

"Then I found out that Miss BYU was not eligible to enter the Miss Utah pageant." Because the previous year she'd entered and won Miss Salt Lake Valley, a preliminary for the Miss Utah pageant, she could not enter that local again. Her only other possibility was to compete for Miss Utah Valley. However, because the director of that pageant had resigned, it looked as though, for that one year, there would not be a Miss Utah Valley. At the midnight hour a substitute director was found and the pageant did go on, though it was too late to raise scholarship money for the winner. From Sharlene's point of view, that was not the most critical factor. She simply wanted a second crack at Miss Utah.

She got her wish when, in March 1984, she was crowned Miss Utah Valley. At that point, Sharlene and her parents pulled out all the stops.

With her wardrobe well under way, Sharlene turned her attention to other areas. Understanding the kinds of questions she would encounter in the interview portion of the competition, Sharlene aggressively studied current affairs and international issues. She read books and brushed up on authors, politicians, humanitarians, and other dignitaries. On certain topics that she felt would almost certainly surface at one time or another—the Equal Rights Amendment, the economy, politics, morality, the Church's stand on women, and many others—she outlined point-by-point explanations of her views. "I didn't want to hem and haw about things. I wanted to have issues and ideas clearly outlined in my mind. That's probably one of the best things about the whole pageant. It makes girls think about what they believe, and why. I had answers prepared for all kinds of things—how I'd describe myself in three words, how I felt about President Reagan, what I'd do with the political situation in Nicaragua."

Also, Sharlene's voice tends to get higher when she's nervous or talks fast, so she practiced voice control, making sure she could modulate her voice properly when she talked.

She reworked her talent number after she decided that she had to sing and accompany herself on the Paraguayan harp. "That is very difficult," Robert Wells explains, "because one hand is playing one rhythm and accompaniment while the other is playing a different rhythm and the melody. She worked a long time to be able to sing to the audience and not look at the strings."

And yes, even Sharlene had to worry about her physical condition. Though she's always been slender, even skinny, Sharlene has a tendency towards what she refers to as "saddlebags." Her father elaborates, "She did a lot of running to keep that under control, but at the same time we had to build up her weight so she wouldn't be too skinny. I fed her double-thick milkshakes made with half-and-half cream that I make at home. But at the same time she was exercising every day."

Though Sharlene was definitely the woman of the hour, her father had some uncertain and uncomfortable moments of his own. A lingering question lurked. Should the daughter of a General Authority participate in these pageants?

Elder Wells worried and felt uneasy about Sharlene competing in these pageants. "The Junior Miss competition didn't bother me because there was no swimsuit involved. It was all very modest. When she got to Miss Utah that first year, they calmed me by assuring me that the swimsuit part was held behind closed doors. So I agreed to that. But the second time she ran for Miss Utah, we were told that for the first time in the Utah pageant history a television sponsor was insisting that the swimsuit competition be shown on television. That was the point at which I had to decide if I could allow my daughter to participate in this."

Elder Wells was aware of, and perhaps disturbed by, a

statement President Kimball had made some thirty years earlier, in which he counseled LDS girls to avoid involvement
in "bathing beauty contests." It was a dilemma that repeatedly came to the forefront, and it would not be until the
weeks preceding his daughter's participation in Atlantic
City that Elder Wells resolved the issue to his satisfaction.

"I came to the conclusion that if Sharlene were dressed
in as modest a swimsuit as the swimmers at BYU wear, and
as modest a swimsuit as the Olympic swimmers wear, then
it would be acceptable." Accordingly, when an appropriate
swimsuit could not be located, they hired a seamstress to
tailor one to fit the need. The finished product was a modest,
though flattering, white one-piece double-lined suit that
later in Atlantic City would be referred to as a "Utah standard swimsuit."

"I also rationalized," Elder Wells continues, "that President Kimball had in all likelihood been referring to the
girly-type competitions of years ago, of smoke-filled rooms
and leering men who would watch the girls parade by. The
scholarship pageants of today are like pentathalons, where
the winner is a total woman with the highest point total in
many events. Those who are not just the prettiest or who
have the best figures win.

"I've been concerned about the fact that Sharlene is not
only my daughter, but the daughter of a Church official. I
feel I have reconciled both aspects. I've come to feel that
all of the eighty thousand girls who start out at the local
pageant levels are winners. They gain self-confidence, they
improve their abilities to articulate and perform, they gain
the friendship of other girls, and the experience of having
competed. I think they all win something, and I feel the
pageants are modest and in good taste, with highly moral
people involved at all levels."

By the time the Miss Utah pageant rolled around, things
were on an even keel. Elder Wells had resolved his hesitan-

Sharlene receiving the crown as Miss Utah

Miss Utah with attendants Nancy Ayers (left) and Christie Welch (right)

cies. And Sharlene had studied, rehearsed, exercised, and even eaten herself into the best shape possible, or as she puts it, "I'd fixed myself up the best I could." She was ready to compete.

On June 16, 1984, Sharlene Wells was crowned Miss Utah.

Chapter 9

Reaching for the Stars

"Sharlene and her mother thought she could win," Robert Wells says. "I was skeptical. I figured the judges would either be incompetent or biased."

Helen and Sharlene weren't the only two who felt she had an honest shot at the Miss America title. One Sunday during church Robyn Thompson leaned over suddenly and whispered to Sharlene, "How are you going to carry your harp when you're Miss America?" Sharlene stifled a chuckle, but Robyn was anything but kidding. When asked if she *really* thought her roommate was Miss America material, Robyn says adamantly, "Absolutely, and I told her that. There aren't many girls who are as intelligent and talented as she is, as poised and articulate as she is. She can speak Spanish, play the piano and sing well, and play the harp very well. She may not be exceptional in any of those areas, but in my opinion she was and is the composite girl."

Though Sharlene insists that prior to her second attempt at Miss Utah she'd never thought much about the Miss America pageant, other than the scholarships available, there had been at least one instance where she, perhaps subconsciously, had placed herself in the same category. It had happened when she read an article about Debbie Maffat, Miss America 1983. The story had centered on how diversified and accomplished Debbie was, that she was a fine musician, a good athlete, an excellent student, and so on. Sharlene says, "As I read I kept thinking, 'I can do all those things, too. What's so unusual about that?' It wasn't that I thought I could be Miss America, but those things didn't seem unique to me."

Despite the pats on the back and votes of confidence, it was another matter entirely to contemplate competing against the nation's best, and prospects of participating in the annual Atlantic City gala sent a series of shock waves through the Wells household.

Not only did Sharlene face preparing for Atlantic City, but she was also Miss Utah. The responsibilities associated with that were staggering. Rebecca Simpson was selected as her traveling companion, and for three months the two of them crisscrossed the Beehive State. Rebecca remembers the schedule was merciless. "We had horrendous hours— short nights, long days. Sharlene never griped about getting up early or staying up half the night. She's not a complainer. We visited as many places in the state as we could in that short while, and we met wonderful people who were quite taken with her. I think many people are at first in awe of Sharlene. But, from what I've observed, when they talk with her, they love her."

Rebecca recalls one day when they were high atop an oil rig, where the rednecks all stood in line to pose with Shar-lene for pictures. "They were delighted with her, and she had a ball." On another occasion Rebecca, who counsels with young girls at the request of a grade school principal, told Sharlene about two sixth graders she'd talked to earlier that week who were having problems in school. They came from poor families who couldn't afford the "right" clothes and other amenities that determine the caste system among teenagers; consequently, they were unpopular and felt alien-ated from their classmates. "We were riding along in my car, and as I related my experience with the girls at the school Sharlene didn't say anything," Rebecca remembers. "Finally I looked over and she was wiping tears out of her eyes. After

a few minutes she said, 'I know exactly how they feel. I'd like
to visit those girls.'"

A meeting was arranged, and Sharlene went to the
school and spent an hour or so with them. "Afterwards,
those two girls threw their arms around Sharlene's neck and
literally hung on her," Rebecca says. Then Sharlene walked
them back to their classroom and Rebecca took a moment to
introduce Miss Utah to the teacher. After pleasantries were
exchanged Sharlene said, loud enough for the entire class to
hear, "Thank you so much for letting these girls out of class
to visit with me. They are such sharp, neat girls." Later,
when Sharlene returned to Utah after being crowned Miss
America, *The Church News* requested that she pose for a
cover photo, preferably with girls. Sharlene consented, but
asked specifically that the two girls she'd met just prior to her
trip to Atlantic City be the ones included in the shot. The
three of them appeared on the November 4, 1984 cover.

Getting a girl ready for the Miss America pageant is no
small task, and many individuals played key roles in helping
Sharlene prepare. Some attention had to be given to her
wardrobe, beginning with an evening gown. Not finding
what they needed in Salt Lake City, Robert and Helen
Wells borrowed an airplane (Elder Wells is a veteran pilot)
and flew to Las Vegas, where they located unusual appliqués
among other things for Sharlene's pageant gown—a tur-
quoise chiffon dress adorned with crystals, pearls, and
rhinestones. "Her winnings as Miss Utah helped finance
that second dress," Robert Wells says. "To tell you the truth,
I still like her Miss Utah dress best."

Despite her preparations, Sharlene would find that her
wardrobe was modest in comparison to the competition.
Helen Wells says, "Many girls spend thousands of dollars on
their clothes, which goes to show that the judges look
beyond the exterior. If they hadn't, Sharlene would have

never won. Her clothes were not nearly as elaborate as those of many other girls."

Sharlene continued her enviable weight control program: running and exercising daily to make sure that what she ate ended up in the appropriate proportions, yet downing one of her dad's double-thick chocolate malts every night. Rebecca Simpson says of the girl who eats an entire container of Pringles potato chips at a sitting, "This girl eats. Then as soon as she gets through eating, she goes and has a meal. And then she eats again."

Sharlene continued to pour over everything from magazine articles to the classics, brushing up on current events and spending more time organizing her thoughts and opinions on key issues. She was coached on how to respond to certain questions, including the Vanessa Williams incident. And she made extensive preparations, or at least was pushed to, for her talent number. During the three months between Miss Utah and Miss America, Sharlene was personally coached on the Paraguayan harp by Stephen Allen, director of the broadcasting and film division in the Church's Missionary Department, and a talented harpist. Some twenty-five years earlier, Stephen's father had been sent to Montevideo, Uruguay, by the Church's building division. There he had become acquainted with Robert Wells, at the time a district president in Asunción. The senior Allen had fallen in love with the Paraguayan harp and taken one home for his son to learn to play. Though Stephen hadn't been thrilled with the prospects initially, he eventually obliged his father and later studied in Uruguay for five years. He is a superb harpist.

Stephen Allen sheds light on the unusual Paraguayan harp. "This is an instrument that has no music written for it. All music is learned by ear. It has thirty-six strings, most of which are white. A few are blue and red, and they tell the harpist where his fingers are. This is an extremely difficult instrument to play." He and his student spent hours designing a special number for Sharlene to play in Atlantic City. He too had been convinced that she had to sing as well as play. "As soon as I heard her sing, I knew that was essential. Plus she has very good Spanish. Playing the harp alone would not be enough in Atlantic City."

There were risks associated with attempting such a number on national television. First, with the exception of the metal tuning mechanism, the harp is made entirely of wood. Under hot television lights, that might prove hazardous. The instrument could go badly out of tune and there would be no way to correct it once the performance began. Second, a harpist plays the instrument by using half finger and half fingernail. Sharlene had weak fingernails which kept breaking. "I think Sister Wells and Sharlene tried every nail strengthener in the book," Stephen says. In addition, there was the problem of miking and setting up the harp so that it would look intriguing on television.

But perhaps most crucial, the instrument requires "extreme concentration," as Stephen describes it. "To concentrate on the strings and yet have stage presence and smile at the audience is extremely difficult. It's something I've never been able to master, but Sharlene has that inner something that allows her to do it."

There was, in addition to the obvious risks, an additional challenge. "There was no question in my mind that Sharlene had a legitimate shot at becoming Miss America," Stephen insists, "if we could get her talent number perfect." That, however, called for a demanding practice schedule, one that Sharlene had trouble adhering to. "We absolutely fought about her practicing," he admits. "I told her I had to have a minimum of an hour a day from her, but she was so preoccupied with everything from Young Ambassadors to being Miss Utah to getting a tan that she didn't get in enough practice. Period. To make matters worse, she has *so much* raw talent that it almost worked against her. I've never seen anyone learn as fast. She is bright, bright, bright. Her ability to pick up the harp is far above average, but because of that, she thought she could sit down at the harp for thirty minutes a day and call it good. I knew that that just wouldn't cut it."

Stephen Allen and Sharlene went the rounds about practicing. He was insistent. She was headstrong. Finally one evening he gave his student a heated pep talk. "Sharlene, I don't want to offend you," he began, "but we've got to get serious. There is no question in my mind that you can walk away with the crown in Atlantic City, but if you don't buckle down and give the harp your best practice now, there is no way you'll do your best onstage. You've got to be able to say, 'I paid the price. I was as prepared as I could be.' Then, no matter what happens, you can hold your head high. But I promise you you'll win if you give it your best shot." She did practice harder, though Stephen admits he was nervous when she left for New Jersey because she was still making mistakes.

Sharlene found some time also to work on her diction, walking and turning, and posture, and she got enough sun to turn her fair skin a gentle tan. Her father says, "I personally feel Sharlene was at her most beautiful when she won Miss America."

Because she'd been selected as a member of Young Ambassadors for the second year, her two weeks just prior to the pageant were filled with concentrated, presemester rehearsals that lasted all day from 8:00 A.M. until 6:00 P.M., with few breaks. After one week of the exhausting pace, and at the prodding of others, Randy Boothe pulled Sharlene aside and told her to take the second week off and get ready for the pageant. Sharlene was surprised to be let out of "spring" training, as it were, as all major choreography is set during those ten days.

Randy explains his benevolent gesture. Because the show they were working up was to be taken to southern Europe, it relied heavily on complex dance routines that required time and exhausting practice to execute properly. "Sharlene is tall, and even for a fairly tall guy it's not easy to throw her around without dropping her a few times here and there. She was getting some humdinger bruises. I'd watched Sister Wells handsew all those beads and doodads on that dress of hers. I knew all the other preparations that were going into the pageant, and I thought, 'Terrific, we're going to mar her for life. She'll go back to Atlantic City with bruises up and down her body.' There was a chance she'd be so exhausted that she wouldn't be able to put one foot in front of the other, let alone her best foot forward."

In the meantime, BYU's fall semester began, and Sharlene started classes along with some twenty-five thousand other students. Then, after just a week in school, she left her books behind and, with her traveling companion, Rebecca Simpson, flew to Atlantic City.

"Sharlene was calm on the plane," Rebecca says, "because at that point she was as prepared as she could manage. It was like being ready for a test at school; you can't wait for the test. The adrenaline is high and you're thinking, 'Give it to me. I'm ready.' She really didn't feel she was in competition with anybody but herself."

Over the years, the Atlantic City Convention Center, separated from the beach and the Atlantic Ocean by the famous Boardwalk, has become the home of Miss America and a place synonymous with pageantry and glamour. In reality, it is a domed, cavernous hangar-type building that houses everything from pro football games to mud wrestling and is situated in an old albeit glittery section of town full of Las Vegas-style hotels and casinos.

The Boardwalk is just that, a wide wooden walkway constructed of planks that runs along the beach. It is in and around the Boardwalk and Convention Center that nearly all of pageant week's activities take place.

Sharlene and the fifty other contestants (one from each state, plus the District of Columbia) arrived on Saturday, but it wasn't until the next day, at registration, that she had a chance to size up the competition. "I thought registration was just that, a registration where you sign in," Sharlene remembers. Under the circumstances, she assumed that an attractive but simple dress would be appropriate for the occasion—nothing too showy. As it turned out, *registration* was a formal term for the girls' coming out party, and the press and members of the media were there in full force.

"The minute I walked in I knew I was in trouble," Sharlene says, laughing now about the situation. "There were all these girls in their hats and capes—high fashion. And there I was, wearing a nice little dress. I had no idea we were being presented to the press. In fact, I had something special I wanted to wear on that occasion. But one by one we were announced, and we had to walk up and down the ramp."

Right off the bat Sharlene felt intimidated. "There you are, with the cream of the crop, and I found myself wondering, 'My goodness, where do *I* fit into this?' In retrospect, I think we were probably all thinking the same thing: 'What am I doing here?'"

It was a shaky start, and things would get worse before they got better. The next day, Monday, was unnerving. It was still early in the game, too early to have made friends or to have become comfortable with the surroundings. Nevertheless, that morning all the girls reported to the beach in their swimsuits and prepared to pose for pictures.

"All of a sudden there were all these beautiful girls in their swimsuits," Sharlene remembers, "and I kept thinking, 'Oh, my heavens, look at all these gorgeous girls!' That's when two or three of the girls stood out." Miss Texas, Miss Mississippi, and Miss California topped the list. "All of the photographers clamored for them. If a photographer wanted your picture, he'd call your name. I got called once. There were several who were always right in the middle of everything, and that was hard. So, already, I was finding myself on the outside, thinking the photographers knew who was going to win."

Rebecca Simpson says, tongue in cheek, "You know why reporters weren't responding to her? Because she was Miss Utah, and Utah, let's see, that's a state somewhere in the United States, isn't it?"

With four or five contestants getting ninety percent of the attention, there was plenty of time for the other girls to get acquainted. After her first taste of what she hoped the rest of the week would not be like, Sharlene decided to ignore the photographers as much as possible, do her best, have fun, and make some new friends, which she did with, in particular, Miss Virginia and Miss Indiana. It was after that first night, in fact, that Miss Virginia shared a sincere and alert observation with her newly found friend from Utah.

"I've already picked out the Miss America," she told Sharlene.

"Oh, really?"

"Yes. It's you."

"Oh, come on," Sharlene replied, "you haven't seen my talent or anything yet. That's sweet of you, but I think you have a good chance, too. We all do."

"No," Miss Virginia insisted, "you'll see. I can always pick the winner."

The next day was the first preliminary, the personal in-

In front of United States map with messages from all of the contestants

terview with the judges. By that time Sharlene had made
friends, and had even received bits of positive reinforcement
from other girls, but things in general didn't seem to be getting much better.

The interview was conducted in a small, windowless
room divided by a dark curtain and lit by one bright light.
When the contestant first entered the room, she was not
able to see the panel of judges, who were screened by the
curtain. Sharlene recalls the sequence of events. "I walked

into the room and was introduced. Then I walked past the curtain and there the judges were sitting, waiting for me. A video camera was running. There was one light right in my eyes and two microphones directly in front of me. I could barely see the judges, though they were just a few feet away. But I could tell that most of them glanced up at me, nodded, and then looked back at their papers. I felt as though it was me and the KGB," she says with a laugh.

How time changes perspective! At that moment, Sharlene found the situation to be anything but a laughing matter. The first judge fired the first question. "Why do you want to be a Little League coach?"

"My first thought was, 'Oh, that's a piece of cake.' But I was still so overwhelmed by the surroundings that I just started talking. I hate being redundant, and was I ever being redundant! I said the word *situation* about four times in a row. And while I was talking I was also thinking, 'Oh, you dummy! This is an easy question, and you're talking on and on but not saying anything.'"

Noted free-lance photographer and author Chris Little asked the second question. "Can you name a fictional character who represents huron?"

"I could tell the other judges didn't have any better idea than I did what that meant," Sharlene says. "They all gave him blank stares." Sharlene had the presence of mind to ask, "Excuse me?" He clarified, "Huron means evil."

"I could have mentally sorted through the books I'd read, but I didn't want to waste time thinking," Sharlene says, "so I answered with the first thing that popped in my mind. 'I can't think of a specific character right now, but the *Inferno* represents the situation of good versus evil,' and elaborated on that."

The third judge was a woman who asked about the benefits of being bilingual, and that question was conveniently in Sharlene's territory. She told about her experiences growing up in South America, and about her recent visit to an elementary school in Provo, Utah, where third graders were involved in a Spanish immersion program. "I told them what it had been like to have third graders ask me questions in fluent Spanish and added that I felt it was extremely important to get involved with peoples from other countries."

The fourth question threw Sharlene for a moment. It was posed by prominent sports artist LeRoy Neiman. "Why do you feel that the development of soccer in the United States has not reached its peak?"

"My first thought was, 'You're asking *me?*' But thank heavens I caught myself before I said that. I did mention that I'd been living in Argentina in 1978 when they won the World Cup, but that here in the United States we had three other major sports that conflicted with soccer. I also added that there was an economic factor involved, that in other countries some of our sports are too expensive, whereas all you need to play soccer is a soccer ball and makeshift goals at two ends of the field."

The next query, posed by Sam Haskell, an advertising executive for the William Morris Agency, threw her for more than a moment. He fired a no-win question at point-blank range. "Sharlene, are you pretty?"

"In my mind I thought, 'What?' But I was still trying to be poised, so I answered, 'I've been told that I am.'"

He returned the volley. "Are you pretty?"

"I'm secure in my physical appearance," she replied.

Again, "Sharlene, are you pretty?"

"At that point I broke down and said, 'Okay, yes. What do you want me to say?' Then he laughed and said, 'Well, I think so, too.'"

But Mr. Haskell wasn't finished. His follow-up question probed deeper. "What's the difference between being self-confident and cocky?"

"I got a chuckle out of that," Sharlene says, "because it

was an interesting way to lead into his question. I told him that if you're self-confident, you're secure within yourself and don't need to go out of your way to build yourself up. If you're self-confident you have time to help others. But being cocky is a facade for not feeling good about yourself."

The final question was initiated by singer Pearl Bailey. After a lengthy prologue she explained, "I'm going to name some prominent women and I want you to name the country they're from. The first one is Golda Meir."

"I replied, 'Israel.' Then she said a name I'd never heard of, but it sounded American so I answered, 'United States.' Then she asked, 'Can you tell me something she did?' I had to tell her I couldn't. She quickly responded, 'You mean you don't know who she is?' And I said, 'I'm sorry, I don't.'"

Sharlene was in the middle of that line of questioning when the bell rang. "I really felt as though I'd been saved by the bell," she admits, "but I also walked out of there on a discouraging note and I thought to myself, 'I blew it!'"

Sharlene's pageant hostess was waiting to greet her, and she asked how the interview had gone. "I told her I'd blown it," Sharlene says, "and the woman immediately counseled, 'Don't tell anybody else that you blew it. No one needs to know that.'" Sharlene took the advice to heart. In fact, later that evening, when her mother arrived from Utah and asked her how the interview had gone, Sharlene replied, "Oh, it went great," in convincing fashion. "At the time, I had no idea Sharlene was concerned about her interview," Helen Wells admits.

Later that night, Sharlene replayed the interview scenario for Rebecca, who analyzed the facts and assured her that from the sound of things she had done beautifully. Rebecca did, however, repeat the counsel Sharlene had received earlier. "Don't tell anyone you feel you could have done better. When the press asks you about your interview, say it went just great and you feel good about it."

As predicted, the next day a couple of journalists approached Sharlene and several other girls who were standing together and asked specifically about the personal interview. "There were several girls who said they blew it," Sharlene says, "and I could tell that that comment gave the other girls an edge. It's as though you admit defeat to your competitors."

Throughout the week, the pattern established by members of the media during that first day on the beach persisted. The press room was constantly filled with journalists and photographers who, in order to interview a contestant, were required to submit the girl's name. During the day of the interview preliminaries, Sharlene and Miss Minnesota were standing back from the action. Sharlene remembers, "I watched her stand there by herself for a while, and then I went over to her and asked if she'd been interviewed yet today. She said she hadn't, and asked if I had. I hadn't either. We sat there and watched everybody else get interviewed, one after another. We were feeling a little left out, as though the journalists were the ones doing the picking. It went that way all week."

Nevertheless, Rebecca feels Sharlene kept her spirits high. "Of course, there were some ups and downs. She's human, and she had some anxious moments, but they weren't the high highs or the low lows. It appeared to me that, generally speaking, she was more relaxed about things than were the other girls around her."

Fortunately for Sharlene, the judges were doing the only picking that counted, and it appears that, from almost the beginning, she had an inside track with them. Sam Haskell told her some two months later that she'd been one of the top three interviews. And even Sharlene admits she felt as though the judges were on her side. "Every time I'd look at them, I felt they were looking at me. Yet every time I had to walk down the runway for one reason or another, Miss Texas was right in front of me. Later, when I made the top ten, Miss Mississippi was behind me. All of the photographers were taking pictures of them, never of me. Several times I wondered why it seemed that the judges were looking at me but nobody else was. It made it difficult to keep up my confidence level."

Rebecca Simpson says her own confidence never wavered in the slightest. As early as Wednesday morning, after only the interview preliminary had been held, she placed two calls to Utah—one to her husband, and another to a close friend. To both she predicted confidently, knowing Sharlene was within earshot, that her charge would win. "I

Performing on the Paraguayan harp at the pageant

Walter A. Snyder

knew it. It's not that she was particularly gorgeous in rela-
tion to the other girls. There isn't a girl back there who isn't
beautiful, but some are more refined than others, and you
can pick those girls out immediately. Sharlene was the composite girl."

Rebecca's opinion was based on more than intuition and
insight. In fact, the traveling companions of several other
contestants had already pulled her aside to make comments
such as, "I would like to see my girl become Miss America,
but she won't because Sharlene is going to." Rebecca adds,
"All of them said, 'And if my girl can't win, I want Sharlene
to be the one.' I think they were drawn to Sharlene because
she was so unaffected by everyone else. She didn't let the
other girls and the pageant pressure get to her. She was prepared, she was happy."

One of two pageant hostesses assigned to Sharlene and
Rebecca had been the hostess for Vanessa Williams the year
before. She said to Rebecca, "I have a feeling about this girl.
She could really do it."

Rebecca's outspoken confidence might have seemed pre-
mature, but she insists, "I would not have built up Sharlene's
hopes if I hadn't been sure. I told her she was going to be the
next Miss America, and that she needed to get emotionally,
mentally, physically, and spiritually prepared for the transition, because it was coming."

But first, Sharlene had to get through a number of preliminaries, and that very night her confidence was shaken.
It was Wednesday, the night of the talent preliminary. Talent had always been her stronghold, and, as Sharlene says
now, "I thought if I was going to do anything back there,
they'd notice me in talent." She did perform well. Several
girls told her after she walked offstage, "You're a shoo-in to
win talent." A couple of reporters made similar comments to
Rebecca.

Helen Wells, who has judged pageants herself and understands the point system, tried to objectively—if that was possible—evaluate and rate all the girls, as she'd done many times before. "Many of the other girls sang, and they all had such a similar style that I thought the uniqueness of Sharlene's number plus her execution, which was solid, would give her the nod."

It did not. Sharlene did not win the talent prelim. Helen Wells admits, "I was shaken by that, and I believe Sharlene was too." Sharlene says, "I was disappointed, but there really wasn't anything to feel bad about. I was competing against a lot of talented girls. It wasn't that I didn't have any talent, and I felt I'd done my best." Evidently her showing didn't bother Sharlene too long. Rebecca says she scarcely mentioned it when they returned to their hotel room that evening.

Still, by Wednesday evening, Sharlene's confidence was suffering. As she sized up the events to date, she'd not scored well in the interview; and now, in the talent segment, traditionally her strongest event, she evidently had not been noticed. What Sharlene did not know at the time was that she had scored just one point behind her group's talent winner.

The following night was swimsuit, and everyone—Sharlene, and both her parents—were nervous about that, each for their own reasons. Sharlene says, "I've never enjoyed the swimsuit part of competition. I've always told myself, 'Just try to walk nicely. You really can't hope to get any points.'" She does agree there's no other way for judges to gauge physical fitness. "You should see the judges from our perspective. They look so uncomfortable. They'll look up, then quickly glance down, then look up again. It's not as though they're drooling over all these women."

In fact, Sharlene hadn't had the orientation to swimsuit her competitors had. They, in that instance, had a decided edge. In Utah, that portion of the competition has traditionally been held in private and, if anything, has been down-played.

Swimsuit would not take a backseat in Atlantic City, and Sharlene knew it. That apparently did not intimidate her, however. Though, in an effort to keep their stomachs as flat as possible, most girls refuse to eat or even drink much water the day of the swimsuit competition, only an hour before Sharlene downed nearly half a pound of the famous fudge sold along the Boardwalk. She was not, obviously, overly concerned.

"I knew I was in shape. So I thought that if I was going to walk out there I might as well do it right and be confident. I wanted the judges to look at my face and my smile. Once I walked out there, I concentrated on exuding confidence, even though I didn't feel terribly confident."

The net effect must have been positive—fudge and all. Helen Wells says, "Sharlene appeared to be calm and assured, with no hint of self-consciousness, and her swimsuit was the most modest." Apparently, the judges reacted in much the same way, because when the swimsuit winner was announced, Miss Utah got the nod.

Helen Wells says with emphasis, "I'd give *anything* to have captured on film the expression on Sharlene's face. She was absolutely stunned."

Sharlene indicates just how stunned. "I was more shocked to win swimsuit than Miss America. I don't think I've ever been more shocked to win anything—in my whole life. When he called out 'Miss Utah!' I blurted out loud, 'You're kidding!'"

Helen Wells says her husband may not have been quite as thrilled. "I think Bob was embarrassed that she didn't win talent but that she won swimsuit. I'm sure he wondered how everyone back in Salt Lake City would take it. I believe it was the first time a Miss Utah had won swimsuit, and wouldn't you know that it would be a General Authority's daughter. But then he got a telegram from Elder Durham on behalf of the Quorum, congratulating her in the preliminary win, and I think he felt a little better."

Immediately after the win, Roseann Nielson (who, with husband Norman, cochair the Miss Utah pageant) explained to Sharlene how significant her swimsuit win might be. "The judges probably noticed you in interview," was her appraisal. "But the next night, the talent preliminaries, is the first time they do ballots, and at that point they're still green judges. They don't fully understand how to work things. The winner of each category is not necessarily the girl who gets the highest ratings but the one who gets the most consistent ratings. After they realized you hadn't won talent, they started getting worried, because they wanted you in the top ten."

Whether that philosophy was accurate or not, winning the swimsuit competition had decisive impact on Sharlene's psyche. "As soon as I won that, I thought, 'This just might be my year, my time to win.'"

However, Sharlene kept reminding herself that this was, after all, the Miss America pageant, and there were fifty other extremely talented girls all competing for the same prize. "Yet I've always known in the back of my mind when things were going to go well for me. That's what has helped me determine what to get involved in. When I won swimsuit, I thought, 'They noticed me in an area everyone had been telling me was my weakest.'"

That night, when Sharlene returned to her hotel room, she told Rebecca, "I feel that I'm going to do it." That, of course, came as no surprise to her traveling companion.

Friday night was reserved for the evening gown competition. Winners are not announced for that segment. By Saturday morning, the morning of the pageant, Sharlene still felt cautiously confident.

Saturday is reserved for day-long rehearsals in preparation for the pageant that night. Because announcement of the ten finalists had already gone out over the wire, the girls were asked to relinquish their radios and confine themselves to the Convention Center. A room upstairs was outfitted with comfortable cots and a buffet.

It was a hot September morning, and because rehearsals were the only events scheduled for the day, Sharlene, who didn't feel like curling her hair, donned a baseball shirt and Levis and pulled a baseball cap down over her golden locks. As had been the case all week, few others followed suit. "All the girls back there had a different outfit for every occasion," Sharlene explains. "They'd show up for rehearsals in high heels and absolutely glamorous outfits." As expected, most of the girls were dressed to the hilt when they arrived at the Convention Center that morning. "When I saw everybody," Sharlene says, "I just wanted to say, 'Relax. There's nobody here to look glamorous for.'"

Sharlene wasn't the only one to make the observation. When Debbie Maffat, Miss America 1983, saw Sharlene come out in her casual attire, she remarked to Ellie Ross (Ellie is one of two chaperones who switch on and off every thirty days as Miss America's only traveling companion), "There's your Miss America. That's the kind of girl you want."

Later Debbie pulled Sharlene aside. "I'd never talked to her before," Sharlene says, recalling their conversation. "And I was still thinking, 'Wow, this is Miss America.' She turned her back to everyone else and said, 'You did a great job on your talent, and congratulations on swimsuit. We have our fingers crossed for you.'"

Perhaps the gesture of good luck paid off, because later that evening, as Sharlene and Rebecca made final preparations, they were confronted with an unexpected problem—

one typical among women but rare along Atlantic City's Boardwalk during pageant week—Sharlene didn't have anything to wear backstage. "It was hilarious," Rebecca says. "Everyone saves their most wonderful outfits for the final night, even though they're only seen in them for a few minutes before they change into their competition outfits. But it's an unwritten rule that you can never ever be seen in anything twice, and we were out of clothes."

They improvised. Sharlene had one pair of black slacks she hadn't worn; Rebecca owned a beautiful pale pink silk blouse. "We put those on her, with her pearl earrings, necklace and bracelet, and that was it," Rebecca says. "And you know, when we went out and saw all the other girls, all of their glitter blended to some degree, and Sharlene stood out. I heard several people say under their breath, 'Can you believe Miss Utah? What understated elegance!' We've laughed about that night many times since then."

It's not as though pressure isn't intense during the preliminary competitions of pageant week, but with millions of television viewers and a packed Convention Center during the final two hours of the pageant, things really heat up.

It could be that the announcement of the ten semi-finalists provided as much drama as anything. Pageant officials knew where the parents of all the girls were sitting, and before the show began a representative located Bob and Helen Wells to tell them their daughter had made the top ten. Sharlene, of course, wasn't privy to such information.

As Gary Collins began to read the names, Sharlene was calm. "I knew from past experience that I'd be towards the last, because the finalists perform in the order they're announced, and for some reason judges like to have the harp towards the end." Robert Wells was sure they had read at least fifteen names before Sharlene's was finally announced, but Sharlene couldn't have been happier when her name was read third to last. The placement was ideal. "It's an advantage to be towards the end when you perform," she explains. "The judges remember you."

How did Sharlene feel, preparing to perform on national television with the title clearly within striking distance? She had two things working in her favor that night. First, through the years she's developed a preperformance strategy that works for her. "I used to concentrate and meditate before going onstage. But that does not prepare me adequately, because once you walk onstage your adrenalin starts pumping, and it's easy to lose control. Now I try to get myself psyched up, almost hyper. I jump around, dance to the music others are performing to, and talk to people so that I'm pumped up when I walk onstage. When I walked out that night, sat down and hit the first note, it didn't phase me that I was on national TV."

In addition to her backstage preparation, Sharlene had help from an additional source. Prior to leaving home, her father had given her a father's blessing. "I always bless the children that there will be angels round about them," Elder Wells says. "That's just a phrase I like to use." Later, when the pageant was history, Sharlene would tell her father, "Daddy, when my fingers touched the strings, I felt as though there were angels with me."

Stephen Allen, who nervously sat in front of his television, was thrilled with his protégée's performance. "She played the harp flawlessly, but she did not play her piece as it was planned. The entire number came out different. She had never played it that way before, and she'll never play it that way again, but it was perfect."

Elder Wells explains, "I don't think the Lord necessarily intervened or magnified Sharlene beyond her natural self. I do think the Lord helped her prepare, and I think she was blessed that nothing went wrong in her performance, her interviews, and so on. Her talent on the night of the finals was absolutely marvelous, the best I've ever heard her do it. She did everything just right. Now, that's either phenomenal good luck, phenomenal preparation, or the Lord's help in allowing her to do her best."

Finally, the moment had arrived. Even though Helen Wells felt Sharlene was going to win, she was still worried about a couple of others—Miss Texas and Miss Mississippi in particular.

Onstage, Sharlene was trying to maintain composure. "I was thinking, 'I know I can do it,' but I was also looking up and down at the other nine girls and thinking, 'Well she's talented, and she's gorgeous, and she's beautiful, and . . .' But my mind still kept repeating the phrase, 'No, it's my turn.'"

With all the suspense that such a drama deserves, Gary Collins began the countdown.

"The fourth runner up, Miss Texas!"

"I sat back and relaxed at that point," Helen Wells says.

Sharlene takes it a step further. "Miss Texas was the girl everybody seemed to like. When they called out her name, I knew I had won."

"The third runner up, Miss Minnesota!"

"I was *so* excited when my friend Lauren Green was chosen," Sharlene says.

"The second runner up, Miss Mississippi!"

"When they announced Miss Mississippi," Helen Wells says, "I *knew* she had it."

"The first runner up is Miss Ohio!"

"And now, Ladies and Gentlemen, the New Miss America 1985 . . ." The drum began to roll, some twenty thousand observers sat forward on their seats. The remaining six semifinalists all smiled nervously. After an appropriate pause Gary Collins shouted, "The new Miss America is *Miss Utah!* Sharlene Wells!"

"It was overwhelming!" Sharlene says, trying to find a word to recapture the moment. In a daze, she walked over to

B. Vartan Boyajian

Hugging Miss New York as announcement was made that she was indeed the new Miss America

Suzette Charles, who placed the crown on her head. Then, as the crowd cheered wildly, she walked down the runway, tears streaming down her face. "She cried. She shed real tears," Helen Wells says, amazed to have seen her ever-composed daughter break down. Sharlene counters quickly, "I wasn't sobbing. It was just so overwhelming."

Meanwhile, in the audience, members of the Wells fam-

B. Vartan Boyajian

Sharlene receives the Miss America scepter from Suzette Charles

ily were shedding tears, hugging each other, slapping each other on the back. Robert Wells had tears in his eyes. Helen Wells held her head and said, over and over, "Oh, my goodness! Oh, my goodness!"

"It was almost an unbelievable dream," Helen Wells says months later. "Even though I felt she would win, it was such a tingling sensation to hear Gary Collins shout her name. I'll never forget his words—Miss America is Miss Utah, Sharlene Wells!"

Chapter 10

Miss America, Sharlene Wells!

When Sharlene Wells was crowned Miss America 1985, the world took note. Certainly, the pageant that bestows the title of America's most exceptional miss always makes headlines. Though Sharlene won the diamond-studded crown the same day that Princess Diana gave birth to her second son, she would have garnered her share of column inches and broadcast minutes. But when, just minutes after Sharlene's first news conference, word got out that the latest object of all the attention was a conservative, religious girl from Utah who didn't hedge when confronted with liberal issues of the day, front-page stories started rolling off presses around the world.

USA Today and countless other dailies called Sharlene a "Squeaky Clean Miss America." The front-page headline in a major Swiss paper read, "Mormon Queen *Rescues* American Morality." A *Houston Chronicle* article (17 September 1984), with the headline, "Miss America '85 Called Almost Too Good to Be True," is a typical sampling of the thousands of reports that appeared the morning after the pageant. "Sharlene Wells of Utah projected a squeaky clean image of a twenty-year-old Mormon student who collects soap and doesn't believe in premarital sex, smoke, drink, or gamble. She also teaches Sunday School. 'What a relief,' said one scandal-weary pageant official. 'She is almost too good to be true.' Wells, whose biggest secret just might be that she wears contact lenses, said she is not ashamed of any-

At breakfast with her family right before a press conference the morning after she won the title

thing. 'I'm going to have to think about that,' the deeply religious BYU junior said when asked about past embarrassments. 'I can't think of anything right now. As I have said, I've lived my values seven days a week.'"

As would be expected, every article wasn't a glowing review, but in general, comments were at least fair if not positive. Even *Time* magazine wrote, "Considering the debacle over nude photographs that led to the resignation of last year's winner, the judges' choice of Miss Utah as the new Miss America seems made in promotional heaven. Sharlene Wells, 20, began her reign last week by promising a return to traditional values."

Unlike many of her predecessors, Sharlene was a focal point worldwide. The extensive coverage no doubt resulted from three factors: first, she was born and partially raised in South America, giving her international appeal; second, her endorsement of puritanical and pristine values, highly uncommon in the 1980s, made her something of a rarity;

and third, her predecessor's indiscretions had created inordi-
nate interest in the pageant. Sharlene's story was front-page
news in major papers everywhere from Peru, Uruguay,
Brazil, and Venezuela to France and Germany. In Asunción, Paraguay, where she was born, the headline of that
country's largest newspaper read, "La Paraguaya Que Es Miss
NorteAmerica." She was the cover story on *La Nacion*,
Buenos Aires' verson of *Parade* magazine, and countless
other international periodicals.

Cartoonists quickly offered their wares. One favorite,
published in the *Lexington Herald*, showed Bob Guccione,
the publisher of *Penthouse*, sitting behind a desk, dressed
fashionably with beads draped around his neck and dark
glasses propped on his nose. He's talking on the phone and
says, "Silhouettes of her sipping a milkshake with Marie Os-
mond and two straws? That's all you can get?"

Bob Hope had a good time with Sharlene on his television special (28 September 1984). "Did you hear about our
new Miss America?" he asked his audience. "She's a Mormon Sunday School teacher from Utah, probably the most
wholesome Miss America we've had. She's so religious that
she has stained glass in her compact, and she has nude pictures of Bob Guccione. She says the next time he opens his
mouth she'll publish them in the *Ladies Home Journal.*"

And it appears that mainstream America took interest in
this young woman whose views on life were simple, straightforward, and a throwback to days of yore. Among many letters to various editors and editorials on the subject, one such
reader sent her missive to the *Rocky Mountain News* (27 September 1984). "There is a story waiting to be told about
which every American can be proud. Our new Miss America stated that she has lived a life beyond reproach, which
means no more juicy stories and photos. This is a pretty fantastic claim for most twenty-year-old women to make, but I
don't know a single person who didn't believe her when she

said it. We don't even expect our national leaders to be beyond reproach. How refreshing to have a young lady represent herself in such a way. She didn't hedge or try to diplomatically avoid controversy when she said proudly, 'I'm a Mormon. And that speaks for itself.' It has been so long fashionable to avoid mentioning religion in any public statement. . . . The American people are tired of hanging their heads in shame for the iniquities of their leaders and representatives. Reporters around the country should be lifting up their chins and smiling as they tell the good news. These are the good 'ole days."

On the flip side of the coin, Sharlene's outspoken defense of wholesome values may have irritated or embarrassed others. Some couldn't stomach what they considered to be her Miss Goody Two Shoes act. *The Globe*, for example, wrote (9 October 1984), "Was Miss America Contest Rigged— Rivals Say Rules Were Changed to Ensure a Squeaky Clean Winner."

But Clifton Jolley, a columnist in Salt Lake City's *Deseret News* (20 September 1984), took everything into consideration and put the hometown girl's conquest into perspective. "The first I heard about a Salt Lake City girl winning the title was when a friend of mine from Missouri called to tell me. And to tell me why.

"'After that scandal with Vanessa,' he said, voicing an opinion that has become commonplace in the last few days, 'the judging committee just knew it didn't have to worry about the photos that might turn up of a BYU coed from Utah whose father is a Mormon Church official.' . . . I thought of [his comment] when I read an editorial headline two days later: 'Virtue Alone Wasn't Enough to Win Miss America title.' . . . I found myself being ever-so-slightly embarrassed about what a Goody Goodikins America thinks this year's Miss America is.

"Embarrassed. My stars and garters, what a long way we

have come . . . when a swimsuit performance takes the edge off our embarrassment. The philosopher Immanual Kant suggested that beauty is valuable and valued because it is the symbol of virtue. . . . Which is why I'm feeling a little less embarrassed than I did. . . . I'm prepared to hope that she won the long-established contest on 'virtue alone.' Because that would mean that after all these years, the Miss America pageant finally got it right."

Sharlene has strong feelings about the world's initial response to her. "Because of the situation with Vanessa, members of the press were really watching what would happen in Atlantic City, and I got more publicity than most other Miss Americas. My religion was plastered all over the country, my beliefs were reported all over the world. I think there was a purpose in all this."

In addition to the barrage of press coverage, Sharlene received an onslaught of response personally. Telegrams and letters poured in from all quarters. Everyone from President Ezra Taft Benson of the Council of the Twelve Apostles to President Alfredo Stroessner, the president of Paraguay, sent their congratulations. General Authorities, Senators, athletes, entertainers, young girls, mothers—hundreds wrote, called, or cabled to let Sharlene and/or her parents know how thrilled they were with her victory.

The following are just a few of those messages:

"Your performance on television was flawless. My sincere congratulations to you as Miss America. This presents a great opportunity to demonstrate the wonderful qualities of womanhood which you represent. We will all be pulling for you and praying for the rich blessings of heaven to attend you as you represent all that is best in the lives of young Latter-day Saint womanhood." (President Ezra Taft Benson.)

"I extend to you my warmest congratulations for your selection as Miss America and my pleasure that you re-

Sharlene with her mother and father the night she was crowned Miss America

member with love this Paraguay where you were born and which you paid tribute to with your sensitive musical rendition. Your selection brings pride to all Paraguayans." (President Alfredo Stroessner.)

"We were all so proud to have a Utahn win the title of Miss America. You are truly a tribute to our great state and an inspiration for all young women all over America." (Senator Orrin Hatch.)

"I just want you to know that I was so proud to have been a part of your selection as Miss America. You have all the right qualities to be the best we've ever had. I'm proud of you and what you stand for." (Sam Haskell, a judge in the 1985 pageant.)

"My congratulations to you on being named Miss America! You well deserve the title, Sharlene, for you are the embodiment of all that is right and good and beautiful in American women. You are a breath of fresh air to this world." (Elder Russell M. Ballard, presidency of the First Quorum of the Seventy.)

"Please receive our warmest congratulations for your marvelous achievement as well as our most sincere wishes for a very successful and happy year as Miss America. Many thanks for keeping Paraguay present in your memories by wearing our native costume and playing and singing our music." (Staff members of Citibank, Asunción, Paraguay.)

"I am pleased to offer my sincere congratulations upon your selection as Miss America 1985. It was indeed a wise choice, given your beauty, intelligence, and talents. The Paraguayan citizens residing in the United States were thrilled the moment you started playing the Paraguayan harp." (Martinez Mendietta, Paraguayan ambassador to the United States.)

"The last few years of the Miss America contest were not of the caliber that the Miss America pageant had been in prior years. . . . [But] as the pageant was proceeding Saturday evening, I was especially observant of the interviews, and your intelligent responses led me to root for you as our new Miss America. I was ecstatic when you were crowned Miss America." (An American citizen.)

And they continued to pour in—cards, letters, telegrams, phone calls. Some were skeptical, others critical. But
by and large, the national and international response to
Sharlene Wells was one of relief and one of curiosity. Perhaps the most common sentiment was a very simple one—
"It's about time."

Chapter 11

No Biz Like Show Biz

"I had never really pictured what Miss America did, because becoming Miss America had never been one of my dreams or goals," Sharlene says. "It was just that I'd gotten on a train that didn't stop."

As it turned out, it was an incredibly fast train.

Glamorous. It's the best word that fits the lot of a Miss America. Right? Right—and wrong.

It could be argued, probably successfully, that being crowned Miss America is something akin to becoming a mother. There is no substantive way to prepare for it, no way to anticipate what it involves or will demand, and unfortunately, no easy formula for carrying it out. Being crowned Miss America is an achievement, a mark of excellence; but *becoming* Miss America is a transformation, a "calling," if you will, of unrivaled proportions.

One day Sharlene Wells was a twenty-year-old, penny-pinching albeit lovely BYU coed whose most glamorous "show biz" exposure had consisted of bit solo parts with a collegiate variety show, and the next day she was Miss America—still twenty years old but instantly a celebrity, complete with all the pressures, privileges, and remuneration. She was a "Who's Who" and was expected to perform on cue, display all the social graces, discuss issues of the day with clarity and resolution, and take on a larger-than-life title and social status. It's an overwhelming transition. As she says, "There's really no preparing for it. It's like nothing you've ever done before." Consequently, the opportunity and the adjustment, though glamorous, are taxing.

"Technically, Miss America's contract allows her to work only four hours a day. That's her actual on-duty time," says Robert Bryan, Miss America's business manager. What he doesn't immediately mention is that those four hours do not include interviews of any kind, press conferences, packing and unpacking, luncheons that turn into two-hour events, and travel. "But the day could run much longer," he admits, "and often does. If she is in a town for an appearance and a local talk show wants her on in the morning, we'll book her there for exposure for herself and for the Miss America pageant as well. But that's not counted as part of her working day." When Sharlene was in a large city to make appearances on behalf of one of the pageant's four major sponsors (Gillette, Beatrice, Pillsbury, and American Greetings), she might have been required to make appearances at four different locations for an hour each, even though travel to all four places may have required an additional four hours. It was not unusual for her four hours to turn into ten or twelve.

Miss America can expect to travel over a quarter of a million miles and make over two hundred appearances in one year. She can also expect to earn upwards of $125,000, not including over $25,000 in scholarships and other odds and ends, such as a 1984 red convertible with a Miss America insignia on the door, compliments of an Atlantic City car dealer.

It didn't take long for Sharlene to realize that, indeed, she was on a very fast train—a train that was picking up speed.

When Sharlene finally returned to her hotel the night (actually the morning) she'd won, it was nearly 3:00 A.M.

While she'd been steered through her maze of post-crowning duties, all of her personal belongings had been moved to a luxurious suite in the Caesar's Hotel, and inside there were "tons of people waiting for me. I didn't know who most of them were," she remembers. She would later find out that, among others, they were security guards, pageant officials, and her new traveling companion. "I felt as though I was watching it all from the outside, that it was for somebody else. I kept wondering, 'Is all this fuss for me?' It was strange. All I wanted to do was get on the phone and call home."

The suite was laden with flowers, fruit baskets, and even a well-stocked bar complete with bartender. (After a while someone called the bartender aside and asked, "Have you had much business?" He replied, with a curious look on his face, "I haven't had any. I can't understand it.") Security guards stood watch outside her door. "We all felt like Dorothy in the *Wizard of Oz*," Helen Wells says, "suddenly thrust into a new world, not really knowing what was happening or having the time to find out."

Sharlene didn't have time to do much that night—including sleep. Around 4:00 A.M. her suite finally cleared of well-wishers, and only three hours later her first photo session as Miss America, traditionally held on the beach, was scheduled to begin. At 9:00 she conducted her first major press conference, and later found a moment to say good-bye to her parents, not realizing it would be some time before she saw them again. The race was on. "I had no idea what to expect. But then I started looking at my schedule, which absolutely covered one calendar, and I said, 'Hold it, when do I go home? You mean, I'm out here forever?'"

Not forever, though it might have seemed that way at first. Her itinerary read like a bus schedule. New York. Boston. Miami. Portland. Los Angeles. Chicago. Detroit. Miami. Jacksonville. Honolulu. Dallas. And everywhere in between. It would be almost two months before Sharlene had a chance to return to Utah, and then it would be only for her two-day homecoming. In the meantime, she was a news-making celebrity with her first stop in New York City and dates with the national media. On Monday morning following the pageant, Sharlene appeared on the "CBS Morning News," "Good Morning America," and "The Today Show." All three proved to be routine, if appearing on national television can be described nonchalantly. She also granted her first live radio interview with the largest CBS affiliate in New York City, and in doing so got a hands-on indoctrination to what she'd face throughout the year.

"I was warned that this particular reporter was known for really putting the people he interviewed on the spot," Sharlene recalls of that experience, "so I could only imagine what was coming." As predicted, the journalist quickly questioned and even criticized Sharlene's views on everything from the Equal Rights Amendment and abortion to her support of President Reagan. His attitude was unmistakably condescending. "You know how reporters try to throw you off by looking around the room while you're talking and appearing to be disinterested?" Sharlene says. "He did that. For the first twenty minutes or so he appeared to be totally bored."

Sharlene ignored the interviewer's manner and jumped in with point-by-point explanations of her views on the subjects he raised. On the question of the Equal Rights Amendment, for example, she argued, "It's a vague, eighteen-word amendment that we have no idea how the courts will interpret. I don't know about you, but I don't want to be susceptible to the whims of a judge. Furthermore, the Fourteenth Amendment already gives women the rights they need. If we were to start giving rights to every minority or special interest group in the country, we'd be in big trouble." As the minutes ticked away, the reporter shifted less and less in his chair. After awhile, his attention was focused directly on

On the set of "Good Morning America" with David Hartman and Joan Lunden

Sharlene. His last on-air comment was, "I have to admit that you're the most intelligent Miss America I've ever met, and I respect you and admire you for your opinions."

Robert Bryan says Sharlene handled the Eastern press with skill. "She amazed them, especially with her Spanish. One reporter in Atlantic City threw some Spanish at her, and she answered without hesitation. Her answers to even the toughest questions were intelligent and complete."

Elder Wells was pleased with his daughter's media savvy. "She's fearless in facing the press. I believe it stems from the fact that she honestly believes her opinion is as valid as any-one else's, regardless of their credentials. She has enough dignity that she doesn't let the press abuse her. There seems to be something about her demeanor that brings respect from them."

Sharlene says there was motive in her madness. "It's true that I didn't leave anything to the imagination, but I felt the only way I could deal with reporters was to be completely

honest with them. They're so used to having people hem
and haw and give safe answers, that I knew I had to know
what I was talking about, or they'd eat me alive. Otherwise,
it would have been too easy for them to take pot shots at
someone like me who defends high values."

Through it all Sharlene retained her sense of humor, and
even giggles about the silliest question she can remember.
The first night in Atlantic City a reporter asked what her favorite vegetable was. "I was so floored by it that I couldn't
even think," Sharlene says. "Then I remembered—green
beans."

As time would roll on, questions from reporters would
run the gamut, from the absurd to the sublime. By and large,
the media would treat Sharlene fairly, probably because she
diffused them up front with her candor and charmed them
with her humor. Midge Stevenson, one of her two around-
the-clock traveling companions, says, "I think many people
were more impressed with Sharlene than they thought
they'd be. Some were begrudgingly impressed. She didn't
hedge on answers. Some were startled to find themselves
hearing such conservative views from a modern young
woman."

Meeting the New York press was only one aspect of Miss
America's first trip to the Big Apple. Having gone to Atlantic City with little more than the clothes she competed in
and a few other odds and ends, she hardly had the wardrobe
suitable for a Miss America. To remedy the situation, Midge
Stevenson took her to three carefully selected shops in the
Garment District.

Inside each store, clerks hurried to bring outfits for Sharlene's consideration. Dresses, sweaters, furs, shoes—there
was no end to the glamorous merchandise. "One dress would
be $250, another would be $200, and I kept saying, 'This is
great. I'll take it,'" Sharlene remembers. "Soon my traveling
companion realized it hadn't dawned on me that *I* was pay-

ing for these things, and she said tactfully, 'Now, you may want to be selective about what you really need and what travels well.' Then it all clicked, 'Oh, I'm paying for all this. Then, I'll take that *one* dress.'" Sharlene laughs even now as she remembers those first naive days. (On her first shopping spree she purchased three dresses, several sweaters, a mink coat, and an all-occasion raincoat.)

A few other things dawned on her during those first few days as Miss America. "Right after I won it seemed as though everyone was taking care of me. My traveling companion was doing my packing. For those first couple of press conferences someone came in and did my hair and makeup. I was still so amazed about everything that I wondered, 'Wow, am I going to get this treatment the whole year?'" Sharlene pauses before she exclaims, "Not hardly!"

Quickly Sharlene got a dose of the highs and lows that come with celebrity life: the expectations, the criticisms, the responsibilities, and the fast pace. Within the first few weeks of her reign she spent two days in photo sessions for Simplicity (for a Miss America pattern book), attended ribbon cuttings for condominium and bank grand openings, appeared at a trade show in Hawaii, taped a segment of "Family Feud" (Sharlene led a team of former Miss Americas against a Mrs. America team. "Last year the Miss America team lost every game. This year we cleaned up," she says with relish. "We won $42,000 for CARE"), ran in Northwestern University's Alpha Delta Phi five-mile run, did a phone interview with a Paraguayan radio station, interviewed with many of the country's major magazines, appeared at dozens of conventions and banquets, signed thousands of autographs, posed in an endless series of photo sessions for pageant sponsors (including one for an aerobics album plugging Pillsbury's Figurines diet bar), and appeared and performed on the "Tonight Show" and the "David Letterman Show."

She quickly experienced the dichotomy that befalls every celebrity. Some people love you; others don't. In her case, much of America felt she was the best thing since Chevrolet, motherhood, and apple pie, but others found her squeaky clean image unpalatable and consequently looked for her faults and made noise about them.

"I received plenty of bad press. Some reporters made fun of me," Sharlene says simply. "One of the worst articles I read originated in Seattle and poked fun at everything from my patriotism to how goody-goody I was. Then there was a

Posing for an exercise album for Pillsbury's Figurines

derogatory article published in a magazine in Great Britain. Neither of those writers had met or interviewed me. And then there were the critics who said I wasn't good looking enough to be Miss America. Over and over again I heard the comment about having a nose that's three feet long."

Helen Wells says she doesn't remember anyone suggesting before that Sharlene had a big nose, that her hair was atrocious, that she wore the most awful clothes. But then, pre-September 1984, Sharlene's looks were not a topic of conversation. However, Miss America's are, and from day one, the question of whether or not she was pretty enough to be Miss America surfaced repeatedly.

One such comment originated on a West Palm Beach radio station, where, shortly after the Miss America pageant, one disc jocky had a field day with everything from Sharlene's nose to her morals. Some weeks later Sharlene was in West Palm Beach, and the same radio station invited her to do a live interview. The conversation went well and after some time the disc jockey remarked, "When you won, as you probably know, there were D.J.'s on this station who criticized you because of your nose, but your nose doesn't look big to me." Both he and Sharlene laughed, and just a few minutes later one of the station executives walked into the studio, sat down, and motioned that he wanted to talk on the air. "I've been driving into the station while listening to this interview," he began, "and I just want the whole listening audience to know how impressed I am with our new Miss America. She is beautiful in person, and we publicly apologize for the derogatory remarks broadcast on this station." Several months later the same West Palm Beach radio station invited Sharlene to participate in an alcohol awareness program, for which she gave a fifteen-minute phone interview, expressing her views on the dangers of drinking.

Despite the criticism, Sharlene found no reason to apologize for her appearance, not that there was reason to.

In fact, photos rarely do her justice; she's much prettier in person. On the other hand, she never represented herself as the most beautiful girl in America. As Robert Bryan says, "Miss America doesn't have to be a stunning knock-out; in fact, you can always find a prettier girl than the one who wins. But if a beautiful girl can't handle the press and speak intelligently, what good is she? Miss America is supposed to be the composite. Talent is very important in the selection process, and the interview is perhaps even more so. Miss America has to be that unique combination."

"When I talk in person with members of the media," Sharlene says, "I can almost always change a negative opinion of me. Otherwise, they take what they consider to be my goody-goody morals and have a heyday with them."

Experience is a demanding teacher, and even in person, things didn't always turn out as she might have liked. When the reporter and photographer from *People* magazine arrived for their interview, Sharlene asked if she shouldn't at least put on her shoes before having photos taken. Her feet were tired and suitably adorned with Dr. Scholl's medicated disks. The photographer insisted he was aiming for a head-and-shoulders shot. Her feet wouldn't even be in the photo. Several weeks later, when the appropriate issue of *People* magazine hit the stands, Sharlene was aghast to find a full-length photo of her, dressed in a snakeskin-like dress, and with nothing on her feet but the Dr. Scholl's pads. The pose was less than flattering and led Blackwell, the California designer, to include her on his "1984 Worst Dressed List."

Sharlene was embarrassed about the *People* photo and Blackwell's dubious distinction, though she took his nomination in relative good humor. "There I was with Joan Collins and Victoria Principal, and they look terrific. Actually, I thought it was an honor." Robyn Thompson remembers a phone conversation she had with Sharlene shortly after Blackwell's list was announced. "We were kidding her about the list, and she said, referring to Blackwell, 'Oh yea, pretty nice guy, huh?' That's one thing about Charlie—she's a handler. She plugs away at things and doesn't complain. I've seen her misunderstood and criticized by friends and ward members at BYU, many of whom thought she was conceited. I've never seen that in her, but I know that and other things about her reign have bothered her. She's never been one to talk about it, though, or to drag her friends into her problems and complain about people. It's not her."

Aside from how well she did or did not dress, or how big her nose was or wasn't, another annoying question cropped up in conversations with journalists, and after a while it grated on Sharlene. The question was the inevitable. Did your membership in the Mormon Church have anything to do with winning the title? And how did the Vanessa situation affect all that?

The first time she addressed the first question, in her first press conference immediately following the pageant, she had answered, "I certainly hope so. I live my religion seven days a week."

In time the incessant insinuation wore thin. "I started thinking, 'That's not the only reason I won!' It didn't seem that I was getting much credit for the talents I do have. The recurring implication was that I didn't win fair and square, the same way every other Miss America has won. My self-confidence suffered."

It didn't take long, though, for Sharlene to rebound. "I finally decided, 'So what?' Yes, I did win, and I do feel confident about my abilities and talents. But really, my values *do* reflect everything I am, everything I can do. My values have made me what I am. So if they are the basic reason I was able to win, then so be it."

As far as what pageant officials discreetly refer to as "the Vanessa situation" was concerned, Sharlene was forthright about her views. This, considering her pronounced defense

On the "Tonight Show" with David Brenner

of morality, surprised some, such as David Brenner, the "Tonight Show's" guest host who interviewed Sharlene on the late-night talk show. When Brenner asked her directly about Vanessa, Sharlene admitted that she agreed with pageant officials on the action they'd taken in asking her to step down, that the dignity of the title was at stake. But she drew a clear distinction between Vanessa the woman, and Vanessa's mistake. "She is a talented, beautiful woman, and she was a tremendous Miss America," Sharlene clarified. Brenner, surprised by her response, replied, "You just said something that's very good. Many people might think that, being a Mormon and all, you'd have a more myopic view of the whole thing. And that speaks well of you."

By now, the train was moving ahead at full speed and it took the passenger a while to get used to the schedule. "You just don't know what you're getting into," Sharlene says. "It's wonderful, but it's also tough. A lot of people think that somehow you spend all your time floating around in a bathtub, but it's not that way at all. It's a lot of work."

Her first couple of months as Miss America went by in a blur. Rarely did Sharlene spend more than a day or two in any one city. It was one supermarket opening, speech, autograph-signing party, real estate project ribbon cutting, reception line and dinner party after another.

The endless autograph-signing appearances came as a shock at first. "Try signing your name as fast as you can, while trying to make a courteous comment to someone you've never met, and do it for four hours non-stop," Sharlene challenges. After her first try at it, Sharlene returned to her hotel and flopped on the bed. "It was draining. I kept thinking it was dumb to be so tired, but I was pooped." Autographs were but the tip of the proverbial iceberg. "Every appearance was different, and I was always a little edgy about what would be coming next. It was *work*, and I was exhausted. They said I had a four-hour appearance limit, but that got to be funnier as time went on."

The first dose of exactly what kinds of things a celebrity, any celebrity, is inevitably exposed to was revealing to Sharlene. "At first I wondered if I was accomplishing anything. I'd go from place to place, make an appearance, shake hands and smile, and sign autographs. That was all I had to do. It was hard to accept the fact that people weren't coming to see me because of *me*, but because of my title. The Miss America title is an institution. Some people just wanted to touch me. At first, it all seemed a little superficial."

She also found there was plenty of pressure, that it wasn't easy to be scintillating, warm, and wonderful day after day. "Miss America is *always* onstage, and it took me almost six months to figure that out. You really can't let up or not be gracious, even when you're dead tired. It's almost as though I was the hostess at every single event, because everyone wants to talk with and be made to feel comfortable by Miss America."

"Everyone" included close friends and relatives, some of whom found it difficult to understand why Sharlene was suddenly inaccessible, even to them. Robert Wells says, "Those few who had a chance to be with her, to pop popcorn or talk or go snowmobiling with her, found that she was still her old self. But it was difficult for some to understand why they were not able to have free access to her when she was in a certain city, and there may have been family and friends who felt she was being egotistical and was not interested in them. But her time was not her own."

Case in point. One friend in a certain city asked her if she wouldn't make a brief appearance at church to a group of young girls. Sharlene understood she was simply to poke her head in and say hello to a few teenagers. But when she arrived at the airport (after a five-hour flight), local Church officials were waiting to rush her to her hotel. "What for?" she asked. "You must change into a gown and your crown. Everybody's waiting." Trapped, she accommodated, and found a full production waiting at the church, where she was expected to sing, talk to the group and sign autographs. It was late before she returned to her hotel.

"It was a full day's work," Robert Wells explains, "especially after spending half the day on the plane. But it was difficult for most people to understand what kind of pressure and time commitments she was working with."

The throngs of people who *do* catch a glimpse of the reigning Miss America at some time during her year in office don't usually understand the hectic pace she keeps. Few realize that, unlike *every* other major pageant winner, she is on the road, nonstop, for twelve months. The travel schedule alone is merciless. It's like having jet lag for twelve months.

The night she appeared on the "Tonight Show," Shar-

lene left straight for the LAX airport and a 1:00 A.M. flight
to Dallas. She had two hours of sleep before she arrived at
her first appointment the next morning. "People kept coming up to me and saying, 'Didn't we just see you last night
on TV?'"

During one grueling stretch, she worked in seven cities
in as many days, traveling during the daytime, making appearances at night. One evening, she arrived at a reception
where she was to greet several hundred people. She was, as
she puts it, "ready to crash," but she put on her appearance
smile and went out to face the multitudes. One woman who
came through the reception line said, "You're so bubbly and
friendly, you must have just come from home or a relaxing
vacation of some kind." Sharlene says, "I felt as though I was
going to collapse at any minute. If I hadn't been so tired, it
would have been really funny."

That's not to say that, even during those first two or
three crazy out-of-the-frying-pan and into-the-fire months,
Sharlene didn't thoroughly immerse herself in her role. She
soon found that in her position she had unexpected influence and the power to affect lives.

At a major reception in Sacramento, one woman who
came through the greeting line stopped long enough to ask,
"Is there any way you could come out and sign my son's
cast?" Sharlene said she'd be happy to, but that she couldn't
leave her post until she had a break, which would be another
hour and a half. The woman paused as though making calcu-
lations in her mind, then said, "That would be fine. If you
could sign his cast then, we'll wait."

Ninety minutes later, when she got a breather, Sharlene
went looking for the woman. "I went outside into the hot
sun. This woman had driven her station wagon around near
the door, parked under a tree, and her son, who was in a full
body cast, was lying in the back of the car. I felt so bad. He'd
waited in that heat for almost two hours for me to come out.

It amazed me that it was so important for him to have me sign his cast. I felt that I made a difference to him."

The young boy was typical of thousands who were anxious to have some form of personal contact with Miss America, but perhaps the most anxious fans were waiting back in Utah. In late October, some seven weeks after the pageant, Sharlene made her first visit home.

It was an official visit—Miss America's homecoming— and Salt Lake City, BYU, and the Church went all out to welcome home one of their most famous daughters. Her three-day visit was packed with everything from press conferences and a parade down Salt Lake City's Main Street, to a private meeting with President Gordon B. Hinckley, a fifteen-stake fireside at BYU's Marriott Center, and a luncheon sponsored by the Primary, Young Women, and Relief Society organizations. Sister Kimball, numerous wives of General Authorities, and other dignitaries gathered at the luncheon to hear the success story.

In her address to the audience, Sharlene revealed an incident that had come to have unusual meaning to her, particularly in light of the turn of events in her life. "I was reading in the Doctrine and Covenants about eight months ago when a scripture popped into my mind. I wasn't sure why, but I felt it was very important. The scripture was D&C 30:11. It reads, 'And your whole labor shall be in Zion, with all your soul, from henceforth; yea, you shall ever open your mouth in my cause, not fearing what man can do, for I am with you. Amen.' As I have confronted the press and people from all over the country, I have approached everyone with the idea that the Lord is with me. I have nothing to fear."

She concluded, "I don't feel I have arrived. I still have many goals I'm reaching for. I'd never lean back and say, 'Okay, this is it. I've reached the top.' It's a means to an end. At the end of the year when it's all over, it will really be just beginning."

Chapter 12

Life in a Fishbowl

After three or four months on the road Sharlene settled into a routine. "Things hadn't become dull; on the other hand, nothing phased me anymore. I wasn't always worrying about what would be coming up next." Experience is a demanding teacher. "At first I felt that my privacy was being invaded, that I was being abused, even. There were so many inconveniences. But most of life is an inconvenience, if you think of it that way, and if that's the case, life is a drag. Believe me, life is anything but a drag."

With any anxieties under control, Sharlene picked up her pace. "It dawned on me that I didn't know how often I'd get back to Orlando or Rochester or Miami, so I started working in as many extracurricular activities as possible." She ran, and in this case the word is used literally, to Orlando's Sea World during a spare two hours, where she hugged Shamu the whale and got a backstage tour from Shamu's trainers. She celebrated a February Christmas in Bowling Green, Kentucky, when her hosts prepared the traditional celebration with all the trimmings; donned a flight suit (which she pulled over a sequined gown) at a Washington, D.C., gala honoring astronauts; threw out the first ball at the National Jr. College baseball tournament, including a full windup from the mound; and took up golf (her coach was backup BYU quarterback Steve Lindsley). During a stay in Jacksonville, Florida, she found rare moments to indulge a favorite pastime; she went sailboating on the St. John's River. On

Taking time out to enjoy a little golf

the unusual mornings when she didn't have to be up early, she got up anyway. "I wasn't going to sleep through my year." She learned to deal with cocktail parties. "Sometimes I'd feel a little conspicuous when I was the only person in the room drinking a 7-Up. But when I'd get that twinge of embarrassment I'd remind myself that I wanted to be unique."

She started learning to be, as she describes it, "cheerfully flexible," something that does not come naturally to her. Typically rigid in maintaining a schedule and in dispatching a given assignment, Sharlene found it impossible to maintain any semblance of routine when she was not the one booking her time. "I've always been a very scheduled person," she told *The Saturday Evening Post* (June 1985). "And at first I was frustrated by an itinerary that kept changing.

Obligations would be added to my day to the point that I found I had very little time for myself. It's like a concentrated public-relations job for a whole year, and it requires a lot of mental preparation."

In May 1985, after eight full months on the job, she outlined a typical schedule to a *Florida Times-Union, Jacksonville Journal* reporter (May 27), "Yesterday was Chicago. We got up at 2:30 A.M. and came down here. Tomorrow I think it's Tampa. Then to Salt Lake City, and that will be hard because my family and friends will be right there but I won't get to see them. There's not much free time at all—no time to be with friends and family."

In addition, her fluctuating schedule cut into personal commitments. "For example, I couldn't plan on reading the scriptures every morning, because sometimes I'd have to get up so early that I'd need to read them the night before, and then other days I'd miss altogether." She did learn to use an hour here and there to advantage. On the plane, she'd pull out her tiny Book of Mormon and read, or write in her journal.

Sharlene did not let her schedule affect some of the bare-bone necessities of everyday life. "Ever since I can remember I've gotten on my knees and prayed at night. Three or four years ago I realized I needed to pray alone in the morning, in addition to kneeling in family prayer. I've never been able to go to sleep without praying first."

At one point, when she felt she was getting rusty academically, Sharlene picked up an English honors reading list on a rare swing through Utah (and BYU) and was halfway through *Return of the Native* just a day or two later. She also used in-flight time to keep up with thank-you notes and current events, and that proved to be a blessing.

In May, she was scheduled to be interviewed on a Boston television station. "The commentator was a charming and very intelligent woman, a black woman," Sharlene remem-

bers, "and before we went on the air we chatted for a while
and she asked me all the usual kinds of questions."

When the program began in earnest, the woman quickly
switched gears. "The Miss America Pageant claims that
theirs is a scholarship rather than a beauty pageant," she
began, "so let's see if Sharlene Wells has some brains to go
along with her beauty. Let's talk politics."

Sharlene gulped momentarily, but she immediately accepted the challenge. "She asked me what I thought of President Reagan's visit to Wittenburg, which was big news
then, and I told her I admired his courage and convictions in
refusing to back down under media pressure. She didn't
agree with me, but we had a fabulous discussion. She asked
me about apartheid and Nicaragua and lots of other touchy
issues. It was fun." Evidently the commentator enjoyed it as
well. Later she went on air to say how pleasantly surprised
she'd been at Sharlene's political savvy.

As Sharlene toured the country, similar reports filed in
from all corners. George P. Almond, president of GPA Associates, Gillette-Papermate, wrote, "I want again to say a
heartfelt thank you for your being with us in Dallas. This was
the seventh annual banquet we have held, with many of the
same people in attendance for all seven dinners. There is no
question that for all these people and myself your performance was the best ever. There were numerous comments
about your poise, your warmth, your talent, and of course
beauty. Your hard-working charisma made a good dinner
extra special."

T. P. Strickland, chairman of Benchmark Carpet Mills
from Cartersville, Georgia, wrote, "I want to personally
thank you for the outstanding performance displayed at our
Dallas and Atlanta shows. I congratulate you on being the
most professional Miss America that Benchmark has ever
dealt with."

The publisher of the *Hanford Sentinel* in Hanford, California, wrote, "During my years as publisher of *The Sentinel* I have been involved in many different community events and have had opportunity to observe the reaction of our community to those events. I can recall very few activities that have created as much interest, excitement, and positive reaction as did Sharlene's visit. Rarely have I seen anyone able to deal with the press as easily and straightforward as did Sharlene."

Charlie Welch, longtime director of the Miss Oklahoma pageant, told Sharlene after her participation in the state pageant there, "I've never seen a Miss America handle the press as well as you do."

Hundreds of pieces of correspondence from chairmen of the board, entertainers, politicians, and others reported on Sharlene's effectiveness as a representative of and spokeswoman for America's young women. At least in part, her diversified and semi-aristocratic upbringing may have helped her handle sophisticated and even impromptu social obligations like an old pro.

Sharlene was scheduled on one occasion to make an appearance in behalf of the Salvation Army at a convention in New Jersey. Just prior to the event two inches of snow fell, and as Sharlene describes the scenario, the storm "stopped the world." Transportation halted, speakers cancelled, and with little notice Sharlene became the convention's keynote speaker.

During one of many stops in Chicago, she was invited to a celebrity dinner featuring actress Florence Henderson, who was there complete with a thirty-two-piece orchestra. Midway through the evening Sharlene was asked to sing a number or two. "I talked with the conductor, and we worked out some things without any rehearsal. I had to play it all by ear. I got through it, but it's nothing like what you see on

'Love Boat,' where singers jump out of the audience and swing into a perfectly orchestrated number. It was fun, but scary."

Even a Presidential inauguration wasn't considered complete without Miss America in attendance; as a result, Sharlene, with her mother and father, attended President Reagan's inauguration in January 1985. Though bitter cold resulted in a last-minute cancellation of the inaugural parade and the outdoor swearing-in, Sharlene did attend the inaugural galas held that evening at different locations throughout the nation's capital, and those set the stage for some unforgettable encounters.

When she walked into the VIP room at one of the balls, she immediately tugged on her mother's sleeve and whispered, pointing to one corner of the large room, "Mom, look! It's Muhammad Ali. I've got to go meet him."

Without a hint of self-consciousness, Sharlene made her way over to the former heavyweight boxing champion of the world and introduced herself. Within seconds Ali had motioned for photographers, and as they got set he instructed Sharlene, "Put out your hand and make a fist." She followed directions and he continued, "Now hit my nose. Not very hard, just tap it lightly. We'll get pictures of this." She did and they did, and Sharlene admits she loved every minute of it.

About then, a number of Olympic medalists, including Julianne McNamara and Steve Lundquist, entered, and soon Sharlene found herself in the middle of their group. They swapped stories, photographs, and compliments. "I had the greatest time talking with them," Sharlene says. "One of them said to me, 'You know, you're just like us.' And I said, 'Well of course, we're all just normal people.'"

Sharlene met Olympic gymnast Peter Vidmar one evening when they were both in Salt Lake City. He was giving a halftime performance at a Utah Jazz basketball game, and

Her meeting with Muhammad Ali at the Inaugural Ball

midway through the third quarter he sought her out, and they got acquainted. "That was a thrill," Sharlene says. "He handled autograph requests so well and was gracious with everyone."

It was at the White House Easter Egg Roll that she caught up with Olympic swimmer and medalist Rowdy Gaines. The two hit it off, so to speak, and after their wooden-egg-signing duties were dispensed, Sharlene challenged him to a racquetball match. There happened to be a YMCA close to the White House, so they returned to their respective hotels, changed into appropriate attire, and made their way to the gym. "Rowdy had his USA jacket on, and as we walked to the YMCA he kept getting stopped for his autograph," Sharlene says. "He'd sign, then pass the paper over to me and ask them, 'You want Miss America's autograph, too, don't you?' It was embarrassing."

Rowdy shouldn't have been so magnanimous. Sharlene beat him two out of three games—one in sudden death. (Actually, Sharlene found more time for racquetball than any other sport during her reign. When she'd find herself with a couple of free hours in the afternoon, she'd locate a local club and get a court. She was on the June 1985 cover of *National Racquetball,* and made friends with the magazine's editor, Jean Sauser, an eight-year veteran of the pro circuit. During stops in Chicago Sharlene would call Jean for a game. Sharlene occasionally "scored a few points" off her experienced opponent.)

On another occasion, she and former Olympic decathlon gold medalist Bruce Jenner were guests at a luncheon in Anaheim. As she introduced the number she would perform, Sharlene commented, "I need to tell you what an honor it is to meet Bruce Jenner. I was just learning how to set up the hurdles down in Argentina when he won the gold. He's always been a hero of mine." Sharlene says, "It has been

Sharlene in her NASA uniform talking with children at a Young Astronaut Benefit in Washington, D.C.

fun for me to meet athletes whom I've admired for years. I guess I'm still a sports nut."

She caught up with other heroes as well, including astronaut Don Lind, who escorted Sharlene and her parents on a personal tour of the Johnson Space Center in Houston, Texas. The entourage went inside mission control and toured the shuttle simulator, which was usually off-limits to civilians. Sharlene enjoyed herself immensely. "I had no concept of what the space shuttle was like. The quarters are small, considering the astronauts live there for days at a time. They sleep on bunkbed-type beds, where one sleeps on the top side and another on the underside of the same bed. In space, no matter which position you're in, you feel as though you're right side up. It all seemed so adventurous."

As Miss America, she became acquainted with one "Who's Who" after another. At the NBC Parade of Stars in Los Angeles, she met such people as Bill Cosby, Michael Landon, Meredith Baxter Birney, and David Hasselhoff of "Knight Rider" fame. As the year progressed, she met such people as pro quarterback Joe Theismann and his wife Kathy Lee Crosby, Olympic ice skater Elayne Zayak, actress Sandy Duncan, Vice President George Bush, Gary Collins, Olympic gold medalist Greg Louganis, Utah senators Jake Garn and Orrin Hatch, and Senator Paula Hawkins from Florida. She was introduced onstage, and later visited backstage, at the Grand Ole Opry, and during a stopover in Boston she made connections with the Young Ambassadors, who were on their way to Europe, and performed with them there. At the invitation of Nancy Reagan, she was one of six judges to select nine families to be honored by Mrs. Reagan at a White House reception as part of the Great American Family program.

Perhaps the highlight of the year was a brief visit to the Oval Office the day after President Reagan's inauguration. When Senator Orrin Hatch realized Sharlene had missed attending the inauguration, he arranged for the next best thing—a personal audience with the President on the following day. As it turned out, their meeting was brief, but it left an indelible impression on Sharlene. "He was wonderful," she says, referring to the most powerful leader in the free world. "There was a feeling of awe and reverence in that room. I told him I was proud to be an American with him as our President. Then Mom and Dad came in, and Mom told him we prayed for him every night. He seemed to really appreciate that. Before I left, I thanked him for taking time to meet with me, and he said, 'Oh, that's one of the great things about being President, getting to meet you.' It was a thrill!" (As Senator Hatch and the Wellses waited in an anteroom to the Oval Office, the Senator mentioned that displayed in a prominent location were the Bible and Triple Combination given to the President by the First Presidency of the Church. President Reagan also pointed to the scriptures when everyone assembled in his office.)

When Senator Hatch asked Sharlene who else she'd like to meet in Washington, she answered without hesitation, "Bob and Elizabeth Dole." Whereupon, Senator Hatch ushered the Wellses into the Senate Majority Leader's office, where Senator Dole received them. After the appropriate introductions were made, Senator Hatch told his colleague that Sharlene would very much like to meet his wife, Elizabeth, and asked if he would call her.

The call was made, and though Secretary of Transportation Dole was right in the middle of negotiations regarding the sale of a major railroad, she stepped out of her meeting long enough to rush over to the Senate Office Building. Her command performance may have been, in part, a testament to Senator Hatch's influence, but Sharlene had drawing power of her own. In her first press conference as Miss America, when she was asked who she admired most, she had named both President Reagan and Elizabeth Dole. Sharlene

Sharlene's meeting with President Reagan

later found out that, after she'd been whisked away to New York City for her first appearances, Elizabeth Dole's office had tried unsuccessfully to make contact with her.

Helen Wells recalls the meeting with Elizabeth Dole. "She rushed in like a whirlwind, kissed her husband, who had to leave for a meeting, good-bye, and apologized for keeping us waiting. But you'd have thought she didn't have another thing in the world to do than meet Sharlene. She was personable and personal with Sharlene, talking about the times she'd visited Utah and how much she'd loved it. Though she was only with us a few minutes, she made us feel so important. It was a treat for all of us."

Though meeting President Reagan was definitely the highlight of the year, and rubbing shoulders with any number of other well-knowns was fun, interesting, and even educational, Sharlene found that it was through her interactions with mainstream America she could have the most impact.

At an elementary school in So So, Mississippi, population 150, where Sharlene participated in a patriotic show, the students all wore T-shirts boasting, "I sang with Miss America."

At a hospital in Ogden, Utah, Sharlene visited a boy who had been seriously injured in a freak tractor accident and was confined to bed. He was in great pain and very discouraged about his condition. Sharlene spent considerable time with him in his hospital room and subsequently kept in touch.

The Sunday of General Conference, Sharlene was in Chicago, and it was there that she viewed proceedings in a local stake center. Afterwards, the stake president approached her to ask if she had time to visit a young lady who had recently been diagnosed as having bone cancer and had had her leg amputated at the hip. Sharlene made a trip to the girl's home. She failed to mention the experience to her parents, but some time later they received a letter from President Willard Barton of the Wilmette Illinois Stake that read, in part, "The girl's mother reported to me that Sharlene treated her like a blood sister and acted as though they had known each other all of their lives. They sat on the couch and held hands. Sharlene gave words of comfort, love, and encouragement. I am very grateful."

Throughout the year such letters poured in, giving a day-by-day barometer of how America was responding to its Miss America. A woman in Oconomowoc, Wisconsin, wrote, "As you seem to realize yourself, you were probably chosen because they were looking for your type, someone with no skeletons in the closet! But don't believe that was the only reason. You are very good-looking, talented, and, last but not least, not afraid to speak out on your moral values, which sometimes can be hard to do with so many contrary opinions surrounding us." From a father of three girls, "You have become my three girls' idol and role model. I can't express how much your achievement has helped with my oldest daughter. We have been trying to adjust her ideals and examples to a more wholesome nature. Your recognition has provided that opportunity for change. You are now held in deep respect and admiration by her. Thank you for being such a wonderful person."

Susan Hammett, America's Junior Miss in 1982 and a friend of Sharlene's from that pageant, penned her observation. "You are the best possible representative for the all-American young woman! God definitely has big plans for you, Sharlene! I think that the Miss America pageant had really changed in the past few years, but with you they are back on track."

Jake M. Godbold, the mayor of Jacksonville, was taken with Sharlene. After their visit he wrote, "We have had many renowned people come to Jacksonville, but your visit was a highlight for us! You are a charming and talented person and a perfect role model for our young people today. We are all very proud that you represent this wonderful country of ours."

One woman, a member of the Church from Seattle, wrote to Elder Wells, "My daughter and I had the privilege of attending a fireside where your daughter spoke. I can't tell you how great an impression Miss America made on my twelve-year-old. On the way home she said, 'I really believe I can do whatever I want.' She is a shy girl and I was thrilled to see her new estimation of her capabilities."

One teenage girl wrote, "You've made me realize that it doesn't really matter how popular you are or what you look like. It's as though you're an answer to my prayers, because when I see you and read about you I grow a little more. I hope I can develop some of the outstanding characteristics you have."

Helen Wells collected boxes full of letters from those across America who met and talked with Sharlene. In par-

ticular, people seemed to respond enthusiastically to her
when she spoke and performed. She, in turn, favored the
appearances that allowed her to do one or the other—or
preferably both.

Senator Orrin Hatch thinks Sharlene's influence was
and is significant. "Sharlene is not just a beauty pageant winner, she is representative of today's young women all over
the country. With her articulate ability to express herself,
she's going to have long-range influence. I'd go so far as to
say that Sharlene Wells, through the firm stand she's taken
on moral issues, has done as much to combat the E.R.A. as
those vicious battles we've fought on the senate floor, because she's made it clear that you don't have to be for the
Equal Rights Amendment to be for women."

"It's amazing to me the impact one person can have on
individuals, on groups of people," Sharlene says. "I had to
continually remind myself that I was representing the
United States, the Church, and myself. But I love talking
about goals, trying to motivate others. It's very satisfying."

It was also satisfying to have the subject of the Church
brought up in one way or another on numerous occasions.
Though Sharlene left nothing to the imagination as far as
her values were concerned, she was very careful not to im-
pose her religious beliefs on others or appear to speak in behalf of the Church. But many people made inquiries anyway, particularly on talk shows. "Whenever listeners would
have a chance to call in, I'd get asked about the Church,
especially our views on different things. I never had anyone
call in and say something unkind about the Church. The
comments were always positive, and were usually something
like, 'Our neighbor is a Mormon and we think he's great, but
why do you believe this or that,' and I'd have the chance to
explain what I believed. I wish I'd gone through the MTC
first, though."

Her influence for and in behalf of the Church appears to

have been far-reaching. In conjunction with the 1985 April General Conference, mission presidents from around the world gathered in Salt Lake City for instruction. Elder Wells says every time he shook hands with a mission president for the first time, Sharlene's name would come up, and that from all reports her reign had dramatic influence in several ways.

"They told me Charlie has created an awareness that we are not an oddball, weird sect," Elder Wells says. "Sometimes we're confused with other groups, such as the Mennonites. People remember the pioneers, Brigham Young, and polygamy and often think we're still dressing like Mother Hubbard. So evidently, Sharlene has become a source of conversation.

"Second, because she's conscientious about stating the full name of the Church, it gave the missionaries an opening to talk with people and explain that we are Christians. Each time she was in a new area she got some press. The missionaries said that for two or three weeks following her visit people would talk about her, and that helped them. They said there were nonmembers who were looking for a role model for their kids, and now they've got somebody.

"And they told me the effect she had on the members was electrifying. A lot of members are embarrassed to let people know they're LDS. But Sharlene was very vocal about saying, 'I've got a right to live my life the way I want to live it, and this is how I want to live.' When she says, 'This is how I believe,' there's no way to refute that. Sometimes Sharlene is so outspoken that she startles me a little, shocks me a little. But she gets her point across, and the members respond with a new sense of pride."

There were times when Sharlene felt comfortable in speaking boldly for the Church. After a fashion show in Des Moines, Iowa, which a number of missionaries (on prep day) attended, Sharlene went bowling with the zone. Several investigators went along, and she spent time with each, bearing her testimony and challenging them to earnestly seek the truth. "In instances such as those, I could afford to be direct and do so without offending."

As Miss America, Sharlene may have gotten away with any number of things, but she also got strong doses of excitement—excitement bordering on danger. She remembers the night she huddled in the basement of a Nebraska hotel, waiting out tornado warnings while violent twisters raged only a mile away.

At 11:00 one night in an Atlantic City hotel, the fire alarm sounded. Sharlene pulled on her Levis, her chaperone raced in the door shouting, "Grab your mink," and they dashed out. The fire was on Sharlene's floor, and the next day local papers showed her congratulating the firemen for saving her life, "which was a bit dramatic," Sharlene says.

One evening in New York City, she and her traveling companion Ellie Ross were racing in a taxi to an appointment. The vehicle screeched to halt at a stoplight, and two "seedy looking" men walked toward the car. Ellie instinctively reached over and locked both doors, and the taxi driver looked back, raised his eyebrows, and said, "Don't worry. I'm responsible for your life." "That's exactly why we were worried," Sharlene teased.

While snowmobiling, Sharlene left the trail, hit a sudden bump, and ran her machine into a beaver pond some ten feet below. She bruised her ribs, and her legs were black and blue for two months.

After a late appearance in Greenville, South Carolina, Sharlene stopped at a local convenience store. Dressed formally, she was conspicuously out of place, and as she left the store two men followed her. Her driver was able to shake them, but, as Ellie Ross said, "That's the last time you go into K-Mart wearing your mink!"

After the fact, it all seems humorous, and of course there

were hundreds of funny, if not embarrassing, moments. The worst, Sharlene insists, occurred one morning when she arrived at the Dallas-Fort Worth airport. As she stepped into the busy terminal, the four trumpets of the Brunson Brothers blared her arrival. "It was *so* embarrassing! Everyone in the terminal stared at me. Who could blame them. I'd have stared, too, in any other situation."

As much exposure as Miss America gets, she's not exactly a household word. Sharlene's identity, or lack of it, created some humorous occasions. In L.A.'s Westwood, a sign company who'd produced a billboard sporting Sharlene's photograph had her conduct a man-on-the-street survey. In Candid Camera fashion, she stopped passersby, showing them pictures of the ten Atlantic City finalists and asking if they could pick out the reigning Miss America. One in ten spotted Sharlene's photo, though not all of them made the connection. One man quickly picked out Sharlene's photo and said, "She's Miss America." Then pointing to a different photo he continued, "but I wish she had won."

During a stay in Honolulu, Sharlene visited the International Market, where vendors selling all manner of Polynesian wares set up shop. At one booth, the salesman asked Sharlene where she was from. "Utah," she answered. "I've heard good and bad things about Utah." He said, "But did you know Miss America comes from there?" "I know," Sharlene replied. "I'm a good friend of hers." "No kidding!" the man said. "Hey, everybody, this girl is a friend of Miss America," he announced to anyone who would listen. Seeing that the charade was getting out of hand, Sharlene started to laugh, and then interrupted, *"I'm* Miss America." "Noooo kidding!" the friendly Polynesian hooted. Within seconds, Sharlene was the center of attention in that corner of the market.

Not being recognized came in handy. Sharlene met a handsome fellow one evening in the weight room of a Dallas

hotel. Her "BYU #1" T-shirt created a stir, and they ban-
tered back and forth about which team was the best in the
country. He didn't recognize Sharlene. The next day, he
happened to stop where Miss America was signing autographs, and he found his friend from the previous night sitting at the table. "*You're* Miss America? Fabulous!" Sharlene
shot back, "You mean to tell me that after what you said
about BYU you want *me* to give you my autograph!"

There was the governor who knew full well who Sharlene was, and at a formal dinner, finding no flag in the room
for the Pledge of Allegiance, instructed everyone to rise and
face Miss America. "It was humiliating, not to mention sac-
rilegious."

And what if someone gave a parade, complete with the
reigning Miss America, and nobody came. It happened in
Maryland, where Sharlene rode through the center of town
on a convertible. "There wasn't one soul on all of Main
Street!" she exclaims.

After a late-evening appearance in Chicago, Sharlene
hurried to her hotel, hoping to catch some sleep before her
plane left at 5:00 A.M. that morning. About 1:00 A.M., just
as she'd fallen asleep, her hotel suite door swung open and
the lights went on. Startled, she woke up to find a busboy
standing in her room. "Pardon me, but we forgot to deliver
this fruit basket, compliments of the hotel," he said. "At the
moment I was too tired to respond," Sharlene says. "You
sure have to have a sense of humor in this job."

During a visit to Salt Lake City, Sharlene took in a racquetball match with a friend; afterwards, they stopped for a
hamburger. She was sweating and had on no makeup. It was
lunchtime and the place was packed. After five minutes or
so she noticed that the girls behind the counter were pointing her direction and whispering. Soon four cooks came out
from the kitchen and joined the group. Within minutes

everyone was staring at Sharlene and a line of autograph-seekers had formed at her elbow. "I could not get it through my head that I'd better not go out in public unless I looked presentable."

As fun and/or funny as things sometimes were, Sharlene took her share of lumps during the course of a year. After an important appearance for one of the pageant's sponsors in the Midwest, reports filtered back to pageant headquarters in Atlantic City that Sharlene had been curt with VIP's of the corporation sponsoring her. Pageant officials tend to jump when sponsors (translated, that spells dollars) complain, and Sharlene was called on the carpet for her behavior. Helen Wells, who had been informed of the situation first, remembers breaking the news to her daughter. "It was hard for me and hard on her. She'd been working herself to exhaustion and trying to do the best she knew how, and then to hear the criticism came as a shock. Later, as we got to the bottom of the situation, I could see how there could have been some misunderstandings."

Sharlene had arrived at a reception to find a number of other guests there her age. Delighted to interact with peers, something she rarely had the chance to do, she was shortsighted in paying appropriate attention to corporate officials who'd brought her there.

After that incident, Sharlene was fair game. It wasn't long before word about other shortcomings filtered back to headquarters—for example, that she was "always" wearing Levis when she traveled. On an isolated occasion, when she had traveled by private car from one small town in Oklahoma to another, she had donned a pair of Levis. Her only stop was to have been at a small airport, where she was picking up one chaperone and sending off the other. No one outside of her two chaperones and the driver were to have seen her. But the local press had gotten wind that Miss America would be stopping by, and they were waiting in force when the chaperone exchange was made. Sharlene was caught in Levis.

After a major performance, where Sharlene and a number of previous Miss Americas as well as state pageant winners had been scheduled to perform, the report was filed that "Sharlene had been a prima donna. She was upset when her performance was cut to one song." Flabbergasted at the comment, Sharlene explained that she had only asked to know which song she was going to sing prior to going onstage and hearing the first note. "I just wanted to be prepared and go over the words in my mind before I stepped onstage."

So even Miss America has her low moments, some of which are inevitable and relate directly to the fact that a young girl is taken directly from mainstream America, placed on a pedestal, and thrust, without benefit of established ground rules, into a hectic schedule and sophisticated social settings. Sharlene says simply, "Being Miss America is like getting a Ph.D. in human relations. I feel as though I aged twenty years in twelve months."

Helen Wells says, "Make no mistake. Sharlene has faults. To those who don't get to know her, she might come across as polite but not warm. She has some reserve. It's a carry-over from her childhood. I don't know if she's learned how to make other people feel magnificent about themselves. And Sharlene questions things too much. She always wants to know why things are being handled like they are. On the other hand, I was told that the pageant office received letter after letter praising Sharlene as a wonderful Miss America, and we received hundreds of letters from people who met her and loved her. Of course, I'm biased. I just saw a girl out there knocking herself out, just trying to do her best. But I guess you can't get away from the criticism."

It was inevitable that Sharlene, with her impeccably clean image, would grate on some nerves. Her father is direct in his assessment. "Being called to repentance has always been difficult, and though she didn't call anyone to repentance, the fact that she stuck up for unusually high standards implied something. She is not critical of people who live by their own standards. She is not judgmental. But others, hearing her speak so firmly on issues, tend to think she is judging them. I have heard some reactions from the entertainment and modeling professions, those who say they just wouldn't be able to live with a person like Sharlene. We have a daughter-in-law in the modeling business in the Midwest, and she tells us the models there make fun of Sharlene. That's life, and I think Sharlene can handle it."

Sharlene had some moments when she wasn't so sure. "I've never been criticized so much, and it was hard to take. I had moments when I felt that I was a horrible person." But credit her mature attitude with seasoning and a fresh layer of thick skin. "I finally had to realize that I had faults just like everybody else. It's not that I thought I was perfect, but you don't always notice the areas where you can improve until someone else points them out to you. Criticism isn't all that bad. I started working on my faults with the attitude that faults can be changed, and next time I'll do better. I've learned to take criticism better and not be defensive about it. I'm aware that I have lots to work on, and that's okay."

Sharlene also gained firsthand insight into one of the pitfalls of celebrity life. "I've always thought it's petty when people talk about others. But when I see an actress on TV, for example, I'll often think, 'Oh, her hair looks awful,' or something like that. I think it, but I usually don't voice it. Some people voice it. Once you've achieved some kind of celebrity status, people think they have the right and even the responsibility to voice their opinions. It hurts at first, but you have to learn from it, then let it roll off your back."

Keeping close communication with her parents—both Heavenly and earthly—helped. "In some ways I feel as though I skipped out on my teenage years, because I've always been able to talk with Mom and Dad. They're the only ones in the world I can tell everything." Throughout the year, Sharlene called home almost daily. When Sharlene has problems, her mother tells her to "put herself against the wall, then step away, and get a good look at things." "I remember one time when I was down on myself," Sharlene says. "I stepped away from myself to have a good look. Then I started talking with my Father in Heaven about things. I think it's that combination of talking with myself and the Lord that helps me work things out. I don't stay depressed very long, maybe an hour or so at the most."

From both the thrilling moments and the discouraging experiences, Sharlene says there was much to be gained. "I learned a lot about people. Some of those things are good, some are bad. But the single most important thing I learned is that people, no matter who they are, need praise; they need to feel accepted and important. I didn't have any idea when I started all this that mature and accomplished people would need attention, especially attention from a twenty-one-year-old girl. It doesn't matter if you're Miss America or the mailman, everyone has the basic human need of feeling accepted and appreciated."

Through it all, the glitz and the gripes, it appears Sharlene maintained composure and perspective. The purpose in it all became clear. "After I lost Miss Utah the first year people would tell me, 'You should have won it.' But had I gone to the Miss America pageant the year before, I would not have won. After the previous year's problems occurred, it just seemed that this might be my year. I know I wasn't the most beautiful girl who competed, not the most talented, not the most anything. And it's not that I was coming in to save the pageant. I just think it was my time, and that the

Lord has different purposes for different people at different times."

As her father remarked casually to Stephen Allen prior to the pageant, "Maybe it's time that Miss America is a minister's daughter."

Elder Wells now says, "I think Sharlene was uniquely prepared to restore the image of Miss America as an all-American girl. She was not preaching the restored gospel, but she was standing up for the traditional values that are part of the American heritage. I can't say the Lord raised her up for this, I can't say she's been a flawless representative of the Church and these principles. Our constant prayer has been that things would go well. As one of the Brethren said to me, 'It's one thing to be elected, it's something else to live up to it all year long.' But I believe she's been very blessed. We are very, very proud of her and the way she handled everything."

Robyn Thompson thinks that, if anything, Sharlene's year as Miss America humbled her. "When Sharlene won, people wondered if she'd become a sophisticated person who wouldn't want to have anything to do with people back home. But if anything, I think the experience humbled her, because her inadequacies and responsibilities became so obvious. The first time I saw her after she won she looked so skinny, as though she'd been worn to death. It was draining."

On one of her visits home, Sharlene and her mother took in an afternoon movie at a nearby theatre. As they walked over, she put her arm around her mother and said, "I have to stop and pinch myself, to think I've been to all those places and done all those things and met all those people. It seems like it's just a dream. I feel so normal. I just feel like I'm me, like I always have." Her mother answered, "You're still my little girl."

Elder Wells says his little girl hasn't given any signs of

undo affectation. "I don't believe it has gone to her head. She has always been impatient with imperfections, in herself and in others. One thing that does concern me is that she is now used to professionalism. If she goes to a performance and they don't have the microphones right or they've overlooked some details, she tends to be impatient with the lack of professionalism. Most of the world is unprofessional, so she'll have to control that.

"She is a perfectionist, not to a fault, but it could develop to that extent. She like things right. On the other hand she doesn't much care to clean her room or scour the tub. She's not an impeccable housekeeper. She would be if she had a maid to give orders to." Elder Wells chuckles at his comment.

In brief, her mother summarizes, "She's still our little girl, and she is still intact. I believe she always will be. There's definitely more depth to her now, but overall she's still the same Sharlene."

Chapter 13

The Warmth of Paraguay

She couldn't have foreseen it—the stir her performance in the talent competition would raise. When she decided to sing a medley of Paraguayan folk songs and accompany herself on the Paraguayan harp, Sharlene had no idea that the country of her birth would respond wildly to her performance. After all, her medley of the flowing, melodic music was markedly Americanized, and her chances of impressing most any Paraguayan with her harp-playing finesse were, as she puts it, "about like trying to tell Noah something about floods." Nevertheless, Sharlene's pageant performance on international television electrified the people of Paraguay.

One of her first congratulatory telegrams came from Paraguay's President Alfredo Stroessner; one of her first live radio interviews was conducted in Spanish with a Paraguayan radio station; and in a matter of days a letter from Paraguay's ambassador to the United States arrived bearing an invitation: Would she and her parents visit Paraguay, at their earliest convenience?

Pageant officials were wary. Sharlene was, after all, Miss America. What good would come from adding a trip south of the border to her jam-packed schedule? No other Miss America had ventured beyond United States territorial shores. Jet lag would slow her down afterwards. What about safety? Perhaps her time would be better spent closer to home.

There were those who thought differently, however, including the Paraguayan government. Sharlene and her parents were interested in the international implications such a trip might have. The United States State Department, after being informed by Senator Orrin Hatch and Secretary of State George Schultz of the possibilities, saw Sharlene's visit to South America as a public relations tool.

Unfortunately, none of the above-named groups could finance such a trip. Time was slipping by, and Sharlene's schedule, much of which was confirmed long before she won the crown, was quickly filling up. While the wheels of government spinned, Citibank, Elder Wells's previous employer, and Eastern Airlines, the only United States carrier with regular flights in and out of Paraguay, stepped forward. Their two companies would jointly underwrite the expedition. Though the gesture may have been motivated, at least in part, out of respect for Robert Wells, both Citibank and Eastern were confident that the return of Miss America and the Wells family to Paraguay would be a publicity coup.

The full impact of Sharlene's visit to the small South American country can be appreciated best after a quick introduction to the land of Paraguay itself.

Buried deep in the heart of the continent, the exotic and often forgotten Paraguay is one of only two landlocked countries in all of South America. The climate is hot and tropical; those wealthy enough to afford the luxury often run their air conditioners year round. Tourist traffic is minimal, though much of the scenery and terrain is breathtaking. The capital city, Asunción, lies on the edge of a tropical rain forest. Paraguay is small, relatively poor, and a country that seldom figures in international events or attracts worldwide attention. It has, however, one of the lowest inflation rates and most stable economies in Latin America.

Sharlene arranged to use some of her days off in mid-April to make the trip, and it was a beautiful time of year to travel there. It is fall in April in the Southern Hemisphere, and though the foliage is green all year long, in the fall gigantic trees throughout the country bloom with orchid-like blossoms. It's not quite as hot as just a month or two previous, and gentle breezes cool the evenings.

On Saturday morning, April 20, 1985, after a twenty-two-hour flight (including stopovers), Robert, Helen, and Sharlene Wells landed in Asunción, the city where Helen had given birth to Sharlene twenty-one years earlier. Even before they disembarked, there were indications that Sharlene's visit was big news in the small country.

Rather than taxying directly to the connecting sleeve on the air terminal, the Eastern jet stopped at a predetermined spot out on the ramp where photographers were waiting. Everything had been carefully orchestrated. With the Eastern airliner and Asunción's Alfredo Stroessner Terminal providing the backdrop, Sharlene walked down the steps. At the bottom, she was greeted by the United States Ambassador to Paraguay, Arthur Davis, ranking officials for Citibank and Eastern, the deputy of protocol for the Paraguayan government, and nearly two hundred interested observers. "There was no brass band [although a popular harpist, Cristino Baez Monges, and two guitarists played Paraguayan music], but there might as well have been," Elder Wells says with a smile. "My wife and I were sort of shuffled off in the distance. Even though I knew the Citibank officials very well, it was obvious they weren't interested in me. They were fascinated with Sharlene."

Without delay, Sharlene was hurried inside the terminal, where a press conference, complete with cameras and reporters from every major station and news organization in Asunción, were waiting. "Sharlene was nervous about her Spanish," Helen Wells says, "because she hadn't had time to brush up on the language." It didn't seem to matter. Excited after months of anticipation, and momentarily overwhelmed by the enthusiastic reception, she responded to

questions from her hosts with obvious delight. Groping occasionally for appropriate words, she thanked her sponsors
and others gathered at the press conference for making possible her return to the city and country where she had been
born. When she stumbled with the language, she turned
confidently to her hosts and asked for help. "At the time it
looked to me as though they adored her," Helen Wells says.
"Later, the newspaper reports confirmed that."

Sharlene was surprised by the response. "I was thrilled at
how happy they seemed to be to have me there. I was taken
aback by it all. I felt I was representing the United States
and the Church. It was quite a big responsibility, but I was
excited to do it."

The informal news conference at the airport was just the
beginning of four hectic days in Paraguay; and the United
States State Department, still very aware of the potential
diplomatic implications of Sharlene's visit, had advised the
ambassadors to both Paraguay and Argentina, where Sharlene was scheduled to vacation briefly after her stop in Asunción, to roll out the red carpet for Miss America and her parents, and they did so with gusto.

In Asunción, Sharlene and her parents accepted the invitation of Ambassador Davis to stay at the embassy, complete with servants, maids, chauffeurs, and Marine guards
attending to their every need. The Ambassador's daughter
Suzy was a wonderful hostess, filling in for her mother who
had died just a few weeks earlier in an airline crash in
Bolivia.

It was at the embassy's impressive estate that Sharlene
had her first formal interview, a two-hour affair for a television special to be aired after she left Paraguay. "The embassy
in Asunción is a beautiful Garden of Eden type of place,"
Elder Wells describes, "and they filmed Sharlene out in the
gardens, out by the ambassador's aviary, and in different
rooms. It was a beautiful and very regal setting."

The first evening Sharlene and her parents enjoyed a quiet dinner and recuperated from lack of sleep the night before. Meanwhile, every television and radio station broadcast gave extensive accounts of Sharlene's arrival in Asunción, and while she slept local journalists tapped out reports of their impressions of the young United States celebrity who had unique Paraguayan ties. An article published the next morning in the Sunday supplement to *Ultima Hora,* a large Asunción daily newspaper, typified dozens of others. "In addition to being a serene beauty with a certain freshness, Sharlene Wells, who was born twenty-one years ago here in our country, has shown that she is also a person full of vitality, humor, and intelligence. She presented herself with complete spontaneity and was able to articulate her thoughts clearly. Sharlene will take with her beautiful memories of the country of her birth, where she was received with affection and love."

On Sunday evening a fireside was held for the Saints in

Chapel in Paraguay where Sharlene was blessed and later returned to give a fireside as Miss America

Asunción, and the event turned out to be a highlight of the trip "home." As the district president at the time, Elder Wells had supervised the building of the chapel where the fireside was held. He remembers the experience with nostalgia. "The biggest chapel in Asunción was also the first chapel in Paraguay, and it is the same chapel I personally dug trenches and poured cement for. That was back in the days when the members did most of the labor, and I had wanted to set the example. I would work there during siesta time and evenings, and Helen and the children would come and help. It was absolutely great to go back to that building, where I had some blisters and sweat invested, to hold Sharlene's fireside."

Local Church officials expected nearly a thousand to attend the fireside. The crowd more than doubled that estimate, and before the evening was over folding chairs were set up in every available inch of space, including on the outdoor basketball court and parking lot. Cars were parked on lawns and crowds of people filled the building and swarmed outside. "It was wonderful," Elder Wells says simply.

The fireside, held to one hour, had a simple format. Elder Wells introduced his wife, who spoke. Sharlene then delivered a thirty-minute address, once again in Spanish. "Sharlene speaks fluent Spanish and has a perfect accent," Elder Wells says. "Though she does have some gaps in her Spanish, she speaks the language well enough to speak extemporaneously. As she spoke, she'd turn to me every now and then and ask, 'Daddy, how do you say such and such?' Then she'd go ahead. Overall, she did very well with the language."

It had been requested that Sharlene play the harp, and after her address she obliged, though at first her father was hesitant. "This fireside was held on Sunday and in a chapel, and I didn't feel her competition number was appropriate for that occasion." Accordingly, Sharlene played arrangements of two hymns.

But the Regional Representative, two local stake presidents, and mission president who were in attendance all wanted to hear more. Wouldn't she play her competition number? "I relented," Elder Wells says, "but I asked the audience to refrain from applause." Once again Sharlene began to play the harp and sing in Spanish. "It was a strange thing," her father says. "It was a very emotional situation. She reached that congregation through her music. People cried." Tears form in his eyes as he talks about the moment. "I really believe Sharlene's music touched the people more than anything."

At the conclusion of Sharlene's performance, her father spoke briefly, centering his remarks around scripture that, in his judgment, has unusual application to his little girl. First Corinthians 9:24-25 indicates that those who run in a race should run to win, though they seek corruptible crowns.

"Competition in sports or in the Miss America Pageant or in other worldly contests is seeking after corruptible crowns," Elder Wells explained. "In the gospel, however, we seek after incorruptible crowns. Sharlene's reign will end. She has received an honor of men, which is temporary and corruptible. That is not to say that she can't accomplish much good while wearing her crown. Nevertheless, it is the honor of men. In the gospel, we seek incorruptible or eternal crowns."

At the conclusion of the fireside, people streamed to the front to greet the Wellses. "We were almost trampled," Helen Wells remembers. "In Paraguay, it is the custom to kiss on both cheeks, and it was thrilling to see how much the people seemed to love Sharlene." She was presented with two gifts: exquisitely carved wood bookends with a replica of a harp, and a hand-knit sweater.

On the following morning, Sharlene was honored with a

Meeting with President Alfredo Stroessner during her visit to Paraguay

visit to the office of President Alfredo Stroessner, the President of Paraguay. At one time, because he was the ranking
Citibank official in Paraguay, Robert Wells had had occasion to become well acquainted with President Stroessner
and, in fact, maintains periodic contact. "But on this occasion, I was totally unimportant," Elder Wells recalls, chuck-
ling. "President Stroessner was *fascinated* with Sharlene, a
Paraguayan-born girl who had kept alive the traditions of
Paraguay and who had, for some reason, felt that the
Paraguayan harp and a medley of Paraguayan songs were
worthy of competition. That is what absolutely fascinated
the president and, in fact, all of Paraguay." (Throughout her
visit Sharlene maintained, much to the delight of her hosts,
that Paraguayan music was among the most beautiful in the
world. An editorial in *El Diario*, published on April 28 after
her departure, applauded her for reminding the Paraguayans
of the beauty of something inherently theirs.)

"Even when we drove down the street or went shopping,
people stopped and waved," Helen Wells says. "I think the

people in Paraguay were very proud that this gringo, born in their country, had not forgotten them."

After the visit to President Stroessner's office, Sharlene held a formal press conference at the office of Citibank. Sharlene says, "I was so impressed with the questions asked at the press conferences in Paraguay. I was questioned about many things I'd never been asked in the United States."

She was asked her opinion on what the role of men and women in the family and community should be, how a people can become more cultured, how Americans feel about Paraguayans and South Americans, who should be responsible for raising children, and so on. Sharlene was asked to outline the traditional values she talks about so frequently. "I explained that there were three basic values upon which everything else rests. The first is love of God, the second is love of country, and the third is love of family. The reporters seemed particularly interested in that answer." *Hoy*, a large Asunción newspaper, ran a huge headline the next day: "Miss America's Values Are God, Country, and Family."

That afternoon they dined at a luxury hotel on the shores of Lake Ypacari, a lake where many of the romantic legends take place in Paraguayan lore. That evening Ambassador Davis hosted a black-tie reception honoring Sharlene. Asunción's elite were in attendance, and the embassy was outfitted with a full buffet, musical groups, and all of the pomp and pageantry befitting a South American reception.

Sharlene sang and played the harp. Again the people responded emotionally. "Sharlene was so worried about trying to play the harp in Paraguay," Elder Wells says, "because they have wonderful professional harpists there. But people kept saying that it pleased them so much to have an *espigada* [translated literally it means a tall, slender, golden topped blade or stem of wheat; poetically it refers to a slender, blonde maiden] play for them, and she did."

Sharlene had, in fact, had the good fortune of spending several hours on Saturday and Sunday under the tutelage of Cristino Baez Monges, one of the country's most famous harpists. When the Wellses had lived in Asunción, Robert and Helen had frequently dined at the restaurant where Cristino performed regularly. At the embassy reception, Cristino performed a couple of numbers with Sharlene, and he had intended to do so the following evening at a charity ball. But many of the guests suggested to their hosts, "Please, we want to hear Sharlene play alone."

Nevertheless, Helen Wells says one of her favorite memories of the trip to Paraguay is listening to Sharlene and Cristino rehearse together. "He is the epitome of the Paraguayan—simple, sweet, and helpful. He took time from his schedule to help Sharlene, though I'm sure he could have been making money elsewhere. He spent several hours with her, and she was in seventh heaven. Their music was beautiful."

Sharlene crowded as many more activities as she could into Tuesday and Wednesday. Government officials were anxious that she visit the Itaipu Dam, the largest hydro-electric dam in the world and a major accomplishment and source of pride in Paraguay. On Tuesday, a business associate of Elder Wells's from his banking days offered to fly them in his own plane to the dam. By doing so, they were able to land at a government airport that parallels the mammoth engineering wonder, where an engineer was waiting to escort them to view the project. Sharlene says, "They took us where most tourists don't go. We toured the dam from top to bottom, and even saw a turbine from it's beginning through all the stages until it is completed. It was fascinating."

Why did government officials press for Sharlene to visit the dam? Robert Wells explains the significance. "It is very important that Paraguay could produce the technicians and

specialists to do their share on one of the engineering mar-
vels of the world, and it is significant that Paraguay and
Brazil joined forces to complete the project. It has built their
personal self-esteem. The president is proud of it, the people
are proud of it, and they were proud to have Sharlene go
look at it. The press made a big fuss over the fact that she
would take time to visit the Itaipu Dam."

As their engineer-guide escorted them back to the
plane, he pulled Sharlene aside. "I just want to thank you,"
he told her, "on behalf of my countrymen for remembering
our country and loving us. We love you. Thank you for remembering us."

From the Itaipu Dam the Wellses and their host were
only a thirty-minute drive to one of the most scenic spots in
all of South America—Iguaçu Falls, a fabulous series of hundreds of waterfalls spanning some ten miles on the Brazil-
Argentine border. Sharlene took time for some sightseeing.
"It was exotic to be flown in a small plane right in the middle
of the jungle to a spot where we could land next to the dam,
then to go to Iguaçu Falls, which have to be as beautiful as
anything I've ever seen."

When they arrived back at the airplane on the remote
landing strip, a television crew was waiting for Sharlene.
"Throughout her visit," Elder Wells says, "every news program was running shots of Sharlene and reporting what she
was doing and where she'd been. Every newspaper ran front-
page stories and editorials about her visit. The coverage was
incredible."

That evening, President Stroessner's wife hosted a charity ball at the Paraguay Yacht and Golf Club, and Sharlene
was the guest of honor. On the veranda of the hotel, with a
light tropical breeze blowing her hair, she entertained the
audience: first on the harp and singing in Spanish, and later
moving about the area and performing popular American
numbers. "I don't think the audiences there were expect-

Entertaining at a charity ball hosted by the wife of President Stroessner

ing Sharlene to be as versatile as she is," her father says, "and her performance was fabulous. She moved about the people with ease, entertained with confidence, and absolutely loved associating with those people."

Sharlene's presence was significant enough to prompt the foreign minister of Paraguay to remark to Ambassador Arthur Davis, "This is the greatest diplomatic event that has ever happened to our country."

It certainly appeared, from the heroine's welcome and red-carpet treatment, that the people of Paraguay agreed. The country's Director of Tourism presented her with a plaque, thanking her for visiting Paraguay and thereby publicizing travel to the small country and putting Paraguay in the news. Student-body officers from the two universities in Asunción, the University of Asunción and Catholic University, presented her with flowers and a plaque, honoring her as a Paraguayan-born student who had brought honor to the country of her birth. A music association presented her with a song composed for and dedicated to her.

Some of the most touching acts of kindness came from private citizens. One young man, Marino Verdun, who lives deep in the interior of Paraguay, traveled on a hot, dusty bus for some ten hours to present Sharlene with a poem he had written and hand-engraved in leather for her.

Roughly translated the poem reads: Regal American lady of sculptured silhouette, / You honor my people with your graciousness and with your culture. / You have lifted the Paraguayan harp to the height of its warm beauty. / You have decorated the romantic music with its pure beauty. / You reflect spiritual light and have conquered us with your incomparable talent. / You have brought emotion to the world with your tears. / You are an outstanding Christian lady.

"In Spanish," Elder Wells says, "it is beautiful, classical poetry. Those kind of heart-to-heart things happened every day we were there."

Accepting a plaque from Jorge Escobar, the director of tourism for Paraguay

On Wednesday morning, Sharlene said good-bye to her hosts, and she and her parents flew to Argentina for rest and relaxation. Again, the embassy had been assigned to host Miss America and her parents, but the Wellses opted for rooms at the Hotel Sheraton and some privacy.

It was old home week for all three. Elder Wells, who has spent some twelve years of his life in Buenos Aires, says he is more familiar with city streets there than in Salt Lake City. And though Sharlene couldn't totally get away from official duties, she and her parents did have time to sightsee, visit favorite restaurants, take in a movie (*Carmen* with Placido Domingo), enjoy a morning of sailing on the Río de la Plata that flows through Buenos Aires, and shop for leather goods, sweaters, and other souvenirs.

Though her visit to Argentina was purposely low key, she held a Church fireside and visited her alma mater, the Lincoln American School, where she did two assemblies. Her performances (she played the harp, sang, and spoke for both the grade school and the high school) brought rave reviews from students, administrators and, in particular, parents, many of whom approached Robert and Helen Wells afterwards. "Some of our children," the comments went, "are not used to moving around like your children were, and this is the first time outside the United States for many of them. Many are very insecure about being in a foreign country. Your daughter's open approach to how grateful she is for the education she received at this school is so valuable for them to hear."

Late Friday evening Sharlene was the guest of honor at a reception in the American embassy in Buenos Aires. Known as the most elaborate United States embassy residence in the world, it is a large, gilded mansion adorned with marble stairways and gorgeous crystal and silver trimmings. At the reception, Sharlene was introduced and honored. "The whole experience was overwhelming to Sharlene," Helen

Wells explains. "In her mind, she was still Sharlene. At times she had trouble dealing with her celebrity status. Outside the United States, Americans are *so* excited when people visit from home. When we were living in Buenos Aires, Secretary of State Vance visited, and it was so exciting! He was bringing a part of the United States with him. On our trip to South America I watched the Americans respond to Sharlene, both in Paraguay and in Argentina, and they clamored to meet her. As we traveled with her, we saw that people really did respect the crown she wore. It was a big deal to them, and I believe it made them feel, at least momentarily, as though they were home."

"The trip to Paraguay and Argentina was a new highlight," Elder Wells concludes. "It was a trip of many people communicating one on one. It was very simply a sweet and beautiful experience."

•

Chapter 14

An International Miss America

As though jet lag from the twenty thousand miles she traveled monthly and her extracurricular sixteen-thousand-mile jaunt to South America wasn't enough, in early August of 1985 Sharlene and several members of her family left on an extended excursion that would introduce her to two more continents and cultures.

Although the interest Sharlene generated throughout the world may have continued to baffle pageant officials, she was able to accept invitations to visit Japan and Australia. In both cases, the opportunities arose, at least indirectly, because of her membership in the Church.

In previous years the Wells family had become acquainted with a group of Japanese businessmen who regularly visited Salt Lake City. At the request of their good friend and neighbor, Tim Ashida, the Wells family was asked to present family home evenings for the businessmen. Sharlene and her family were glad to oblige and, through arranging for and performing at the family home evenings, came to know these top-ranking executives from Japan.

When Sharlene was named Miss America, many of these businessmen were interested in having her visit their country during her reign. Tim Ashida made contact with Kyoto Advertising in Tokyo, which is one of the most prestigious agencies in Japan. The advertising agency subsequently agreed to sponsor the trips for not only Sharlene but three of her sisters (including Dana) and parents as well.

During their two weeks in Japan, Sharlene and sisters Elayne and Janet performed at several locations, and the family did some sight-seeing. It was, however, anything but a vacation for Sharlene.

"Sharlene probably had the busiest three weeks of her whole year in Japan and Australia," Robert Wells says.

"Definitely," Sharlene interjects. "In the United States I would have had a travel day and then appeared the next day, whereas in Japan and Australia I was traveling and making appearances every day. There wasn't a day that went by, except Sunday, that I didn't perform."

Sharlene's stay in the Orient consisted of a potpourri of activity. She and her sisters entertained at a luncheon hosted by Kyoto Advertising for their key clients and twice at the Tsukuba Expo, a technological and scientific world's fair sponsored by companies and countries from around the world. One evening their performance there, at the American Can Can Review, was attended by some three thousand guests. Sharlene's other principal appearances occurred in

Welcoming ceremony at Tsukuba Expo 1985 where a kindergarten marching band came to welcome Sharlene

Kanazawa, Osaka, and Tokyo. Among other things, she posed for a photo contest and frequent photo sessions, appeared as a special guest at a "Cinderella" pageant where Miss Kanazawa was chosen and where three samurai warriors offered her proposals of marriage, signed autographs, acted for a day as stationmaster of the main terminal in Osaka, addressed the audience during a performance of the Tabernacle Choir in Tokyo, appeared on several television and radio talk shows, held numerous press conferences, and performed at a dinner party entitled "An Evening with Miss America." She, in turn, was honored by kindergarten marching bands, presidents of broadcasting companies and resorts, mayors, and local media. Her sister Elayne told *The Church News*, "Reporters and camera-clicking admirers, who excitedly pointed and whispered 'Miss America, Miss America!' followed her everywhere."

The *Asahi Evening News* (August 21), a Tokyo daily, wrote: "Blonde and beautiful Miss America Sharlene Wells, her tall, blonde, and beautiful sisters, and their good-looking mom and pop are in town, lending considerably to the scenery at the new Otani Hotel. I must say Mr. and Mrs. Robert Wells are to be congratulated on the way they have raised their girls. Sharlene is spectacular. Shortly after their arrival, the whole family attended a small welcoming party given by the hotel. Sharlene was asked to say a few words, but she said she'd rather sing, and then she did, just like a star." *Focus,* Japan's largest circulation magazine, featured a two-page full-color photograph of Sharlene and her sisters.

Helen and Robert Wells believe their daughter increased her appeal among the Japanese people by advance preparation. "To Sharlene's credit, she made a valiant effort to learn some key phrases in Japanese, and they loved her for it," says Helen.

The Japanese culture was an education for the Wells family, whose international experience has been limited al-

Entertaining during her trip to Japan with sisters Janet (left) and Elayne (right) at the new Otani Hotel

most exclusively to Latin America. In Wakura, a resort town bordering a beautiful lake, Sharlene and her mother (who acted as her official chaperone while in Japan) stayed in a hotel suite usually reserved for the emperor of Japan. Sharlene found the experience fascinating. "The suite was filled with Japanese furniture, except for a huge Sony television set in the corner. I tried the mats that everyone sleeps on, and they're wonderful—like sleeping on comforters. The shower was like a big hot tub area with the showers coming out of the wall. We each had our own maid, but we had to get used to them. They would knock and walk in at any moment, regardless of our state of dress or undress. But they gave wonderful service."

At the same hotel, Sharlene and her mother were honored at a formal, fifteen-course , three-hour Japanese dinner, complete with authentic Japanese fare—even octopus. Both dressed in kimonos for the occasion.

"It was a wonderful cultural experience for us," Sharlene says. "The people of Japan are so polite and courteous. From the cold towels you get in a taxicab to all the bowing, ex-

treme courtesy is built into their culture. It's a very disciplined group of people. I loved our time there."

Robert Wells agrees. "I found the Japanese people to be
very hard-working, organized, thorough, and disciplined. I
was impressed with how many people there speak at least a
little English. Whenever we got lost, if we just looked help-
less someone would come up and offer help, and they received Sharlene warmly. We couldn't read many of the news
accounts, but our host told us that every article mentioned
Sharlene's standards and the Church in a favorable tone.
We hope the trip had a positive effect that way."

At the invitation of Church leaders in Australia, Sharlene and her parents flew directly from Japan to the Land
Down Under for a whirlwind tour of the missions there. The
pace was the year's most grueling and left her and her parents
gasping for breath. In four days Sharlene made stops in Brisbane, Melbourne, Adelaide, and Sydney. She gave dozens
of media interviews by day and spoke at youth-oriented firesides in the evenings.

Her father says, "There is a dramatic difference between
what I think Sharlene has been doing the rest of the year and
what she did in Australia. Her trip to Australia was one
hundred percent for the Church, and Sharlene had her best
chance with both the press and in firesides to talk very directly about the gospel."

Michael Otterson is a seasoned journalist whose back-
ground includes work as the business editor of a British daily
and as a political and parliamentary correspondent in South
Australia. He also currently works as the director of public
affairs for the Church in the South Pacific. Mr. Otterson
describes Sharlene's impact during her trip to Australia, setting the stage for the environment she encountered. "Because of the controversial nature of the previous Miss Amer-

ica, and the extensive coverage Vanessa Williams and her resignation received over here, as far as the media was concerned, the story of Sharlene's visit wrote itself.

"The tabloid approach to print media, dealing with the sensational and superficial, is very evident here. The idea of the Miss America pageant finding itself embroiled in controversy was tailor-made for the kind of Australian readership we've got. Conversely, when Sharlene was chosen, she also got more coverage than normal because of the contrast between her and her predecessor. So our objective from a media point of view was to, first, raise the visibility of the Church, and second, to make the point that you can have high moral values and still have fun in life. You don't have to go around in a long, black coat just because you happen to believe in virtue."

Did Sharlene accomplish either or both of those goals? Mr. Otterson definitely believes she did. "Sharlene lends herself to both objectives so naturally because of her personality, upbringing, and training. She is so completely unhesitating in what she says. She doesn't preach, yet she has a marvelous ability to say what she thinks while making people feel comfortable. She is bright. She needed virtually no briefing. Sharlene and her parents have got acres of talent among them."

On Saturday, August 24, Sharlene arrived in Sydney long enough to grant her first interview, with the largest newspaper in Australia, and hop a plane to Brisbane, where the media coverage began in earnest. Before it was over, she would interview with nearly every major periodical in the country, grant dozens of radio interviews, and appear on "Sixty Minutes" and "Good Morning Australia," both of which are patterned after their American namesakes. "From the beginning," Michael Otterson says, "the press picked up the line of her virginity, asking if she was a typical modern American woman. Sharlene was articulate in explaining what she perceives as the rise of middle American values, the fact that it's all right to be moral, and that, in fact, she believes most of America is with her. Her explanations got very, very good response in Australia."

From the beginning, with her first stop in Brisbane, despite the fact that it was Saturday and traditionally a difficult day in Australia to get any kind of press coverage unless the subject is sports related, "we just had page after page of front-page coverage," Mr. Otterson says. "I really didn't think we'd get much coverage on Saturday, but the Brisbane airport was packed with reporters. Just about every news media organization in the state of Queensland was represented. Both of Brisbane's Sunday papers ran front-page stories about Sharlene's values, the standards of the Church, and the fact that she was unhesitating in her stand. Without exception they referred to her as personable and intelligent. Throughout her stay, she got rave reviews."

The headline on the front page of *The Melbourne Sun* read "Sharlene, the Repenthouse Pet." *The Australian*, the country's largest national newspaper, wrote (August 29), "Ms. Wells is almost too good to be true. She is bright, good-looking, articulate and yet says straight out that she is still a virgin. In contemporary society that perhaps makes her less a role model than a throwback, something that does not worry her."

A front-page article in Brisbane's *The Sunday Sun* reported, "Pretty Sharlene Wells has proven that she is a perfect ambassador for the Mormon Church. Talented, attractive, and exceptionally personable, Sharlene is a walking model for today's well-rounded woman." Sydney's *The Sunday Telegraph* wrote under the headline "Charlie Is an Angel," "She's the woman of the eighties. She's young, beautiful, talented, and intelligent. She wants a career and a husband and a family. And she's still a virgin. Sharlene Wells is as American as mom and apple pie, and when she

Courtesy of the Daily Sun, Brisbane, Australia

Sharlene and friend during trip to Australia

was crowned the new Miss America in September last year the sighs of relief from pageant organizers reverberated in the homes of every clean-living, middle-class American family."

Michael Otterson admits that even he didn't expect the enthusiastic barrage of media interest. During Sharlene's tour, he turned down up to twenty interview requests, in a country where "normally we are battling for every line of media attention."

Allan Jones, a popular personality from a Sydney radio station, begged for an interview with Sharlene, even if it was but three or four minutes over the phone. Sharlene managed to squeeze in a six-minute interview while she waited for a plane in Melbourne. At the end of the conversation Mr.

Sharlene and her father take a moment to feed the kangaroos

Jones said, "Sharlene, it's about time someone stood up for moral values, and I want you to know that the majority of Australia is behind you." Mr. Otterson exclaims, "I have *never* heard that kind of comment regarding our Church position on *anything*. We were stunned when he said it."

Jana Wendt, Australia's Barbara Walters, got a crack at Sharlene. Michael Otterson explains that the interview was conducted with Jana in Sydney and Sharlene in Melbourne, though they had visual contact over TV monitors. "You could see from Jana's initial conversation with Sharlene that she was preparing to talk with a dumb blonde. But as she began, and Sharlene responded with concrete answers, Jana's tack changed. When Jana asked, 'Why do you feel it is necessary to tell the world that you're a virgin?' Sharlene answered, 'Because reporters such as yourself ask me.' At least a couple of times, as the interview proceeded, Jana commented, 'You are obviously very intelligent.' She was clearly impressed with Sharlene, and so was the huge corps of press that talked with her. We didn't have a single negative media interview during her entire stay."

It's possible that Sharlene's candid, unbending, and in-formed approach to the media paved the way for positive re-sults. Reporters came prepared with questions on everything from, "Would you give aid to the Sandinista guerrillas in Central America?" to "What is your response to the nuclear peace movement?" "They were trying to establish whether or not Sharlene was a dumb blonde," Mr. Otterson says. "And the way she responded, Sharlene was a credit to her-self, her country, and the Church. Hers weren't deep, analytical answers, but they were certainly the answers of a well-educated and well-informed individual."

He estimates that, in four day's time, the Church re-ceived at least a million dollars worth of publicity in the col-umn inches and airtime devoted to Sharlene. Of course, in the regular course, no institution could have purchased what Sharlene received. Obviously, as Mr. Otterson adds, "you can't purchase ten minutes on a prime time news program. It's much better from our point of view when we have an in-dependent journalist with no axe to grind commenting on Sharlene."

The extensive coverage was not lost on members of the Church, thousands of whom flocked to hear her and her parents speak at firesides geared for youth, parents of youth, youth leaders, and nonmembers in the four cities she vis-ited. On each occasion, the stake centers were packed. Mr. Otterson feels there was good reason local Church leaders decided to allot all of Sharlene's fireside time to young people. "Here was a young woman who had grown up in a minority environment. Frankly, the last thing we wanted, and I'll be blunt, was for somebody from Utah telling Sydney kids how to withstand peer pressure. Our kids would have just laughed. But Sharlene grew up being the only LDS person in her high school in Argentina, and we felt it was a great opportunity to show our youth that they can maintain standards openly and without apology and do so without being labeled a religious fanatic. We couldn't have invented someone more perfect for our youth than Sharlene."

Initially some of the Australian youth weren't as sure. Some moaned, "Who cares about meeting a beauty queen?" But Mr. Otterson says they quickly changed their tunes. "I sat on the stand at all of those firesides and watched the expressions of our kids. They were absolutely thrilled. And since Sharlene left, we've had nothing but positive reactions."

The father of one fourteen-year-old girl says that his daughter, normally an avid reader of novels and other such material, "has had her head buried in Church books since Sharlene left." When questioned about it she told her dad, "I've been thinking so much about Sharlene and what she said about keeping the standards and determining your own life."

While still in Australia Elder Wells visited with a woman who told him this story: "My son has been completely inactive for several years, and he's caused me pain and problems. He didn't go on a mission. He doesn't live the Church standards. I've been praying for him and worrying about him. Out of curiosity he went to hear Sharlene at the fireside last night, and for the first time he's shown renewed interest in the Church. Last night he told me, 'Mother, I'm very impressed. I'm going to change my life and find an LDS girl to marry. I'd like to become worthy to take her to the temple.'"

The reaction to Sharlene Wells, from Church members and national media was, perhaps, surprisingly positive in a country where moral views tend to be fashionably liberal. Michael Otterson analyzes, "It's as though Sharlene touched a nerve. I really believe that here in Australia there are a large number of ordinary parents who would like to know how to handle their children, parents who feel uneasy about their kids' moral values. Yet, they are not able to articulate the alternatives. What Sharlene did was announce openly, 'Of course, you can say no. Of course you can still have fun. Of course you can have values without being reactionary.' She articulated something that a lot of people just quietly wish for."

Sharlene's stopover in Australia was so brief that she personally couldn't have realized the stir she had raised. But those who've had time to evaluate her visit couldn't stop talking about her impact. Her father summarizes, "We felt very, very fulfilled during the trip to Australia. I can't recall ever having greater spiritual experiences with Sharlene. How appropriate for her to finish her reign doing something exclusively for the Lord!" Sharlene adds simply, "I felt as though I was giving something back."

Chapter 15

What Does the Future Hold?

Unlike many who hit the news, achieve notoriety for one reason or another, and eventually fade, Miss America's share of the limelight has specific perimeters—twelve months, no more and, usually, no less. Yet in that fast-paced, glittery year, she becomes used to a certain pace, life-style and even income. The limos and clothes, VIP rooms, and luxury hotels, can become habit-forming. And though, in most instances, her name may not become a household term, it nevertheless gets tremendous play. While some do slip back to relative obscurity after the crown passes on, it's fair to say that, for any Miss America, life will never be the same.

In particular, it's difficult to imagine Sharlene Wells slipping back into the woodwork. While Sharlene's year as Miss America created a fertile environment for growth and exposure, one facet of her personality remained constant—that intangible, pervasive curiosity and drive to try her hand at anything and everything, to push life to the limit.

"I'm like a kid in a candy store," Sharlene admits. "I have to try everything." In addition to the aspirations she had pre-Atlantic City 1984 (to get an M.B.A., to get married and raise a family, to own a business), she was exposed to any number of inviting possibilities during her travels as Miss America.

So just what does Miss America do when she's no longer

Sharlene with Gary Collins as her reign comes to a close

Miss America? Can she slip unobtrusively back into every-day life? Should she even try?

It may take years for Sharlene to answer those questions, though she is still eyeing a Harvard M.B.A., wouldn't mind spending a year or two at Oxford or Cambridge, would like to travel in Europe, and has an entrepreneurial muscle to flex (owning a sports club or resort looks inviting). She wants to coach Little League. Most of all, she hopes to get married and raise a family, and though her goals might not have changed drastically, her ability to achieve them has received a giant shot in the arm.

There will be much more to Sharlene Wells's life than executing a wish list. Fame, fortune, and privilege aren't without cost, and the price, in this case, may be a life unalterably changed. Some of those changes are the stuff from which dreams are made; others bring challenge.

For example, Sharlene's earning potential is almost unlimited. She's already fielded great interest and solid job offers from entertainment executives and others in high-profile positions; and though for much of her reign she categorically denied interest in any number of glamorous occupations, the doors continued, and will continue, to open. "All along, as Sharlene said she was just going to go back and get her degree, I thought that was fine," Helen Wells says. "But I also know what her talents are and what she can contribute. I just wondered if she realized what she was saying. It's hard for me to imagine her slipping into the woodwork."

Rebecca Simpson says that Sharlene won't escape a high-profile life. "Some Miss Americas are forgotten more readily than others, but not Sharlene. She will not be content to call it good with her one year in the limelight. She will not be content to sit back and let everyone else carry the load."

Senator Hatch, in a personal letter to Sharlene, wrote, "Why don't you give serious thought to taking my place in twenty years?"

All the potential is intriguing, and that can be, as her father appraises it, both a blessing and a curse. "Sharlene has had some very interesting offers in the entertainment industry that, if they materialized, could amount to a great deal of money. It's impossible to deal in that kind of environment with those sums of money and not be affected in some way or another, and it's something that worries me a little. Both her mother and I think Sharlene is well enough suited that she can handle these kinds of things, but it's inevitable that she would pick up some worldliness."

Elder Wells speaks from experience. Reflecting on his years as an international banker in South America, he says, "I enjoyed some of the nicer things of life, and it can be very difficult not to become worldly. I understand something about what the world of high-finance can do to someone. If Sharlene chooses to pursue any of those kinds of opportunities, she will have some challenges to face."

Sharlene realizes she might well parlay her year of Miss America earnings into long-term profitability. Midway through her reign, she'd already accepted dozens of speaking assignments around the country for after her reign as Miss America, assignments that usually offer a healthy honorarium. Other kinds of opportunities, such as endorsements, books, and commercials, are inevitable.

What about the money, the prestige, and the earning potential of a young woman who could, in that regard, far surpass even a hard-working, talented, ladder-climbing husband?

"I'm worried about that," Sharlene admits. "I'm going to have to marry someone who is confident enough in his own abilities that it won't bother him if I develop some of my talents. On the other hand, I can absolutely say that my family will always be my first priority. I want my husband to take charge and be the patriarch of the family. I've been asked so many times this past year about equal rights and how I could possibly agree to let a man dominate me. The right man won't dominate. I've also been asked if it doesn't bother me that women can't hold the priesthood. Of course it doesn't! I'm delighted that my husband will hold the priesthood, because *I* get to be a mom! I do hope there are LDS men out

B. Vartan Boyajian

Sharlene on the night she relinquished her crown as Miss America

there who appreciate women who want to make a contribution in the home *and* in society. But I don't want *any* man
to be a Mr. Sharlene Wells. Where my husband goes, I will
go, but once I get there, I want to be free to use my talents.
It's unrealistic, in this day and age, to expect a woman to
confine all of her energies to the home."

Some of those energies, Sharlene thinks, should be di-
rected towards community involvement and getting an education. "I think it's a sad waste when we don't get involved
in our communities. As members of the Church, especially,
we have values that need to be brought to the forefront in
our society. If others are going to voice their ideas, many of
which are strange and even detrimental to the common
good, we've got to get our ideas and strong values out there
as well and make our influence felt."

From what she observed, Sharlene believes mainstream
America is still comprised of moral, God-fearing people

looking for direction—all of which implies strong responsibility to those who can articulately espouse, defend, and
promote good values. "At first, I wondered if a twenty-year-
old girl could accomplish anything," Sharlene admits. "And
though I don't know that I want to pursue a celebrity type of
life, I have a responsibility now. There is a need for people
who are willing to stand up for traditional values. I talked to
the mayor of Jacksonville, Florida, one day at a luncheon,
and he repeatedly thanked me for representing strong morals. I've met so many people who are like that. I have to
wonder if I shouldn't be willing to place myself in positions
where my voice can be heard."

As far as formal education is concerned, Sharlene says
that, for her, it is an essential. "There are so many ways to
educate yourself," she says. "I personally won't be happy
until I graduate from college, and maybe even go further. I
don't feel I can be a good mother and wife if I'm not able to
hold my own intellectually."

About her hopes to have it all—to get married, raise
children, finish her education, venture out on the speaking
circuit, perhaps have her own business, and leave her mark
in the community—she says, "It would be naive to say that
it's going to be a piece of cake. I have big dreams, and why
not?"

Why not indeed. So far her big dreams have led to big
opportunities. Her father believes she is uniquely suited to
finding that elusive balance between a private and a public
life. "She's ideally suited to espouse noble causes, she's articulate, and attractive in her articulateness," he says. "I believe, and I hope, she'll always be useful to the Church and
community. I can see her going into politics. Actually, I can
see her doing almost anything she sets her mind to."

"At the beginning of all this," Sharlene reflects, "I
thought it would be easy to lose perspective, but my goals are
still the same. I understand better what's out there, and I've

learned a lot about people. I love to speak and perform, and I'll always want to be involved in things. That still doesn't change the fact that my family and family-to-be and the gospel are still the most important things to me."

Perhaps one of the biggest eye-openers of her twelve months "in office" was the people she met. "I've observed a lot of lives this past year. There are people in this country who have no direction. There are others who have goals but don't know how to obtain them. So many times I've thought to myself, 'I sure am glad I know where I'm going.' That in itself is difficult. Yet with the gospel, it is possible to understand yourself and your own potential. If I were going to offer any advice to other young girls it would be to be willing to evaluate yourself honestly. There are so many people who let other people decide for them what kind of person they're going to be. Being completely honest with yourself can be painful, but it's the first step in becoming the kind of person you'd like to be."

Sharlene Wells speaks from experience on that topic, having had typical adolescent ups and downs and a crash course in self-actualization. As her father says, in summary, "Sharlene has her own weaknesses and imperfections. She cries, she hurts, she's disappointed, and has unfulfilled ambitions. She has felt ostracized and all of those things anybody feels going through life. She's worried about being too skinny, or maybe too tall for the boys she's been interested in. She has all of the normal feelings and imperfections any of us have."

She also has spunk and spontaneity. She has the confidence that comes from competing in sports, pushing herself to the limit, and succeeding. "I always just tried to beat my own P.R., my own personal record. I was always happy if I did my best, and that has carried over into everything else," she concludes.

In only twelve months Sharlene received the education of a lifetime. She learned about criticism, about people and why they do what they do, and even something about the elusive meaning of life. She found out how strong she was, and where to turn for direction.

"It's a challenge in daily life to really keep in mind the fact that everything should rotate around the Savior. Things would be futile if there weren't that kind of purpose. Why would I even be interested in raising a family or having a career or getting an education if there wasn't anything more to life than what man has to offer? During my year as Miss America I saw some of the best things that man has to offer, and though the experience was fun, it wouldn't be enough for me to base my life on. The whole purpose of life is to grow and progress. But to what? So many people don't know the answer to that question. I'm grateful that I understand what life should center around. That knowledge is more precious than all the recognition, all the awards, all the money in the world. It's what has buoyed me up during times of discouragement; it's what has propelled me to do my best in times of triumph. It very simply means everything to me."

Epilogue
by Sharlene Wells

It is almost impossible for me to put words to my year as Miss America; it was so many things rolled into one. It was the most challenging and demanding year of my life, and, as you might expect, more rewarding than most things I've attempted. It was exciting and invigorating, frustrating and discouraging. I have never had to stretch myself as far, work as hard, or give as much of myself. On the other hand, I have never grown as much.

What is it like to be Miss America? It's nothing like I thought it would be. I know some people imagine Miss America traveling the country with her entourage, getting in a little public relations work in between the bubble baths and appearances where she blows kisses and waves. Believe me, it's just not like that. It's more like spending a year at boot camp! Up early, always running to meet someone else's schedule, trying to be charming and witty around the clock, crisscrossing time zones, and constantly working to please everyone else. Physically, the pace is a killer. Mentally, it's an obstacle course.

There are so many positive things that have come and, I believe, will still come from my reign as Miss America. First and foremost it was a marvelous learning experience.

As I traveled the nation from Hanford, California, to Portland, Maine, and met thousands of wonderful people, I had a variety of reactions to what I saw. I have to admit that I was a little disillusioned at first. I naively believed that all of America was fantastic, and that all people believed in God and had a strong work ethic. I found out that this wasn't always the case.

I did find out, however, that there are truly millions of solid, stable people who live in this country, people who are filled with the spirit of service and brotherly love, people who have foresight and wisdom. Middle America, contrary to what some forms of media and entertainment would have us believe, is still alive and thriving.

Throughout the year, I often performed a number I called "Stand Up, America." In it I talked about my belief in God and about how excited I am to be an American. I can't begin to count how many people complimented me and thanked me for that presentation. It was well received virtually everywhere I performed it. From what I saw, I have to believe that many Americans feel just like I do.

I have learned a lot about myself. When criticism comes and the demands get heavy, you find out what you're really made of. You find out how to dig down deep and how to exercise faith. So many times I have been asked if it isn't difficult representing the country, or the Church. I feel that *every* Church member represents the Church and *every* American represents our country. None of us are relieved from that responsibility. No one lives in his own little world. I believe I am just starting to realize the impact one person can have, whether it's on a single individual, on a community, or on a nation. We have tremendous influence on each other.

Before last September, the BYU campus was essentially my world. I had goals, and I dreamed about doing great things. But in reality I thought I could go only as far as I could see or touch. I didn't imagine that I could have any influence on anything outside my own little world, let alone upon the world at large. Now, after meeting individuals from all walks of life, I realize that those who are successful

Scott Hancock

in life are simply good people who realize that life is demanding, and that it takes hard work. I have come to the conclusion that we all can have great impact on the world around us if we work hard to accomplish all we can.

Halfway through the year, I found myself feeling anxious for the year to end so I could slip back into the woodwork. After a little soul-searching, I realized that this was totally unrealistic and would be very ungrateful of me. The Lord has given me much more than I deserve. Sometimes we have the tendency to think we don't have any talents, or that those we have aren't good enough, and for that reason we sit back and let others make the world go round. For those of us who have the truth to guide us, who understand what life is about and the full meaning of what we're engaged in here, it is inexcusable for us to sit back and let others carry the load. I believe we must all be willing and prepared to share our beliefs with others.

I have learned that everyone is insecure in some way and has needs that can be met by someone else. We all need to feel appreciated, loved, and respected. Perhaps one of the best benefits of sharing the gospel comes from communicating openly with and caring about others. There is nothing that can replace the wonderful effect of open, honest, heart-to-heart communication.

I have learned that there's a huge, inviting world out there, where people are waiting to be taught and loved and inspired. I have learned that we can't afford to be afraid of failure, because we only grow when we are challenged and take steps to expand ourselves and grow. Some of the best things in life come from initial "failures." We simply cannot be afraid of putting ourselves out on a limb. I have also learned that education, whether it be formal or otherwise, is very important. There is no way we can ever be successful for any sustained period of time if we are not competent and sure of ourselves.

I have gained an intense appreciation for my family. One of the great assurances I have is that my parents love and care for me completely. They have supported me, buoyed me up, taught me, counseled me when necessary, and challenged me to do more and to do it better than before.

Finally, and most importantly, I have come to realize more than ever before just how much the gospel has shaped my life. It is my foundation. Everything else would be superficial if I didn't have that underlying knowledge that life is short, that it is purposeful, and that what I am doing right here, right now, will affect what I do for the eternities.